Me, My Selfie & Eye

A MIDLIFE CONVERSATION ABOUT
LOST IDENTITY, GRIEF & SEEING WHO YOU ARE

Janna Lopez

HUMMINGBIRD MULTIMEDIA, LLC

ISBN: 978-1-73275-380-8 (Paperback)

ISBN: 978-1-73275-381-5 (electronic)

Designed by BookBaby Design.

Printed by BookBaby, Inc., in the United States of America.

First printing edition 2019.

Hummingbird Multimedia

2850 SW. Cedar Hills Blvd. #434

Beaverton, OR 97005

www.memyselfieandeye.com

All photos, including cover, are by Janna Lopez,
except page 113: Leandro Crespi

Dedication

For my children: the heart of my being.

For Mark: the unconditional wind beneath my wings.

TABLE OF CONTENTS

Prologue

drift…

drift like snow, or wood, or maybe even a hitchhiker.

branches, or tides, or concrete don't care;

show up, unannounced, with perfect hair,

or don't.

appear in pants too tight

like a jumbo pillow jammed into a case meant for dainty;

regret and denial about time's unkind manner never hurt—

no midlife mirror ever reflected convenience.

Introduction

Turning 50 is a milestone of physical, emotional, intellectual, and spiritual significance. Monumental life changes occur during a range of time before, during, and after. For several of these years I experienced what I thought was depression. I later discovered that the loss I felt, grief and confusion, originated from a place scholars, theologians and philosophers refer to as a "dark night of the soul." While there are elements similar to depression many of the feelings around disorientation were unique in their presentations. Simply stated: I was fucked up.

I'm sharing my story to illuminate that middle age isn't a crisis but an inevitable juncture when one's identity gets pummeled and we're left to manage the subsequent, unnameable grief. For us ladies, factor in associated menopausal chaos and—voila!—we're officially discombobulated (what a funny word!).

After countless attempts to change the sad-sack channel, I finally realized that a pathway beyond a Dark Night of the Soul wouldn't be the same I've dredged through as when depressed. With depression (at least in my experience), counseling held a spotlight into darker corners. I often still felt sad after a session but I had insight. During the midlife phase I reframed from dark night of the soul to *Dark Flight of the Self* (sometimes abbreviated to Dark Flight or simply Flight), I left counseling more lost, because there was an expectation of clarity that never transpired.

When it came to meandering through my Dark Flight, past problem-solving strategies no longer applied and understanding was elusive. There was nowhere to turn, nothing to label, really, no one thing to identify. If I could have, I would have done anything to change it. But I didn't know what "it" was and since it was foreign, the mystery hunkered down, which added to my feeling of being lost. Because I was.

Relief, although minor, didn't emerge until my understanding of what I was in—a Dark Flight of the Self—became clearer. It was a transformational experience, distinct from both a dark night of the soul and depression. I've since learned where Flights originate, and about the long, uncharted process toward a new reality.

* * * * *

After my identity crashed and aspects of who I'd once been became unrecognizable, a simple yet profound activity helped initiate recovery: photographing hummingbirds. I was as surprised as anyone who knew me by how an unexpected, revised identity began to show itself. As a nonprofessional photographer with little knowledge of the technical capacities of a camera, I was able to capture thousands of lovely hummingbird images. Through these moments of presence, and art, and creation, and freedom, and patience (of which I typically have none), I discovered, for the first time in my adult life, a joy deriving from a place I had nothing to do with. The brief glimmers were bright enough to keep me hanging on. Someday, soon I hoped, midlife might feel better.

This book intends to shape words, thoughts, and process for an entirely separate aspect of midlife evolution. The appeal and awareness of a Dark Flight of the Self as a concept may be as unenticing as a low-budget French film shown at a mall movie plex: it is obscure, hard to understand, and has much less commercial zest than the mainstream blockbusters everyone talks about: Success! or Happiness!

The idea is to create a new conversation. So if any of what's shared here resonates with you, perhaps you'll be less alone through midlife loneliness or grief. Someone might be experiencing a Dark Flight of the Self, yet have no idea that's what they're going through. If I'd been aware of what a Dark Flight of the Self was, if I had known it was a thing—an actual, experienced thing—would it have made a difference? Would it have reassured me that I wasn't going crazy? The past few years were lonely and sad and had no discernible qualities other than being constant and unnameable.

Looking at my experience now through the lens of a Dark Flight of the Self, the disorientation, disconnection, and isolation make sense. They also highlight the need for giving a name to the journey of midlife identity loss that both honors and explains the sadness.

I acknowledge that this book doesn't follow a standard linear narrative or structure. I'm speaking as if we're sitting face-to-face—in that sense, conversations take twists and turns. Age references may jump around depending upon the time I wrote the thought or discovery. I only include snapshots of moments, people, or circumstances because it's not meant to be a complete memoir; in fact, I rejected the notion of it being a memoir at all. Is there more to the story? There always is. I selected what seemed relevant to the struggle, issue, and process of identity loss and associated grief specifically during midlife.

I also acknowledge that my daily challenges and search for Self have a realm of privilege. That word may prompt reaction yet it's true. I've been afforded a freedom to lament that many don't have and this story is from the only reference I have as a white, middle-aged, middle-class woman living in Portland, Oregon. There are people from other cultures, races, religions, and socioeconomic backgrounds living different circumstances who aren't afforded the equal opportunities and basic human dignities they deserve. My heart's keenly aware of luck variations when it comes to the social lottery, and the need for proper humility in honoring everyone's diverse perspectives. I believe in the power of shared human experiences.

In the spirit of self-forgiveness (for what you may not yet understand), and self-discovery (of an anticipatory You that awaits landing), together we fly . . .

Before getting started, I want to make some clarifications.

First, the book title. **Me** is a description for the person I know myself to be, a person I've become based on job, title, and roles I fulfill as mother, wife, friend, leader, sister, mentor; it's the identity onto which I most closely hold. The **Selfie** is the version of one's self (because of job title, expectations, and social media personas) that we *project* out into the world; it's the parts of our identities we want others to see. Being able to see or connect with a truer, unfiltered version of one's Self has become increasingly difficult. Midlife identity loss, struggle, and fragmentation are much more complicated because of the Selfie within a Dark Flight. Finally, between the flux of expectations, changing hormones, and identity grief, how did I, at 50 years old, learn to "see" who I am? The **Eye** is the *process* of how I discovered a renewed vision of who I am throughout my Flight.

Something to note: throughout the book I refer to "self" with a lower-case "s" as the person *I think I am*. When I use an upper-case "S" for "Self," I'm referring to the heart/spirit/soul essence of a Me that is independent of my thoughts—the interior entity I am getting to know. (The same goes for "m" in "me" and "M" in "Me.")

Also, while the people and enterprises in this book are real, some names and titles (including those of my children, all those associated with the magazine and its operation and sale, and the name of the publication) have been changed.

Part I
Me

Fear of Flying

Before we go on, I need to come clean.

Once upon a time I was a competent, confident professional woman.

I used to be somebody.

I had a fancy title printed across a nifty business card: JANNA LOPEZ, PUBLISHER.

I was in command—captain of my ship, pilot of my plane, ringmaster of my circus.

Life was a result of ambition, hard work, production.

Or so it seemed.

Until it wasn't.

Until truth discovered that what I was capable of was based on false idealism.

Until the terra firma of my identity decomposed.

Until then, I'd been certain I'd always known Me.

I could count on this—ME.

Until midlife.

I'd been taught that a good book has a narrative arc and comprises the story of a hero's journey. However, how can the idea of narrative arc be applied when it comes to finding one's Self, one's identity, after the loss of that identity? What I describe—a journey dubbed the Dark Flight of the Self—is far from a curved trajectory. It has no discernible form. It's messy. Midlife identity dismantling is hard to grasp, yet common among many who are redefining their lives—or more specifically, who they are in their lives. Before I carry you along my Dark Flight of the Self, I'll briefly describe some of the original concepts associated with the Dark Night of the Soul.

(To give you a heads-up I was told by a couple of trusted early readers that the first few pages of this book were slightly more dense than the rest. However, it was important to lay groundwork for terms and definitions that the rest of the story is based on. If you find yourself drifting, hang in there! It shifts!)

* * * * *

While some have heard the term "existential crisis," there's another similar, yet uniquely distinct, life transition with which fewer people are familiar: the "dark night of the soul." It was only recently I discovered the concept—what it is, how it's specifically different than depression or an existential crisis, yet has aspects of both.

I was having drinks one night with friends, seeking consolation for the sadness I'd been going through, when one of them casually brought up the term and asked if I'd heard it. Vaguely, as a concept, I had. I got the gist; a dark night of the soul was a time when most of what a person thought was true was being questioned.

As a scholarly, theological concept, though, I was unfamiliar with the term. I went home that night and researched. The discoveries were fascinating. The original dark night of the soul concept derived from a Spanish poem, *La noche oscura del alma.* This poem was written by Saint John of the Cross, a sixteenth-century poet and mystic. The translated poem narrates the journey of a soul toward a transcended union with God. It alludes that the destination—God—is wholly unknowable and as such causes dissonance.

Since the poem was penned, many have written books, translations, and interpretations of its intent. The dark night of the soul related to a crisis point in an individual's life when they attempted to reconcile a disparity between limited human capacity for faith and yearning for a spiritual journey toward God. Mother Teresa wrote about her dark night of the soul as she experienced it for over a decade.

The dark night of the soul has evolved into an expression that's broadly applied in many religious, new age, and spiritual tomes as a way to describe a point in a person's life when big philosophical human questions can no longer be avoided. *Who am I? Why am I here? What is my purpose?*

Best-selling spiritual author Eckhart Tolle described the dark night of the soul as "a collapse of perceived meaning in life . . . Nothing makes sense anymore, there's no purpose to anything . . . It can happen if something happens that you can't explain away anymore, some disaster which seems to invalidate the meaning that your life had before. Really what has collapsed then is the whole conceptual framework for your life, the meaning that your mind had given it. So that results in a dark place."

The dark night of the soul feels like something—a mostly known reality including one's identity—is dying, and as a result, there's a rebirth of spirit, or rather, an activated access to one's spirit. (I define "spirit" as the essence absent of thoughts, ego, professional labels, or social expectations.) With this understanding comes an inherent conundrum: *identity loss is the fundamental premise.* You have to lose your self to find your Self. It is meant to stir and is caused by the same thing—a dismantling of one's identity.

I spent too much energy trying to intellectually make sense of the confusion, scrambling to logically find fixes through a problem-solving toolbox that no longer existed. How can one understand the nature of something they're in, when the point of being in it requires one not to know what they're in? In other words, for a personal opening to take hold and give fertility to the right questions or right epiphanies for this life transition to take shape, I had to be at my own low point. I had to reach an internal valley and dwell there a while.

The abyss is a failed connection between knowing who we are and a transitional reality of who we've not yet become. A dark night of the soul, as a place in life, is a relational death of the person we once were, which is why there's so much grief.

I think about the nature of identities and how we construct relationships to our selves. I can now see through the experience that as sucky as it was, it provided what I needed in order to grow and transition into the next phase of my life.

Based on exposure I've had to spiritual and philosophical ideas, it's hard to believe that I'd never encountered the dark night of the soul concept. If I hadn't (and I consider myself somewhat aware), I suspected there were probably many others who hadn't, either. Even so, whispers of connection to places that needed a little love or insight were waiting to be seen, felt, heard, or remembered.

I'm an analytical, pragmatic, mentally driven person. I devote way too much time talking myself into and out of things based on my thoughts, which are often jumbled, stiff, and overpowering. Control of my thoughts, my mind, my ego, and my identity helped me move forward in life. But they've also kept me trapped.

Then one moment of one day, I was unwillingly shoved out of the nest of all that was familiar to my mind. On the other side of a trapped yet known realm of who I was in the world was a vast, internal terrain of an unfamiliar, strange space.

* * * * *

In order to break the entrenched spell of familiar, something SO big, SO concrete and SO identity-shattering had to occur to ensure an utter decimation of my relationship to who I thought I was. While I was in (what became) the onset of a Dark Flight, to ease my weary mind, I talked with a lot of people to make sense of the non-sense. The more I talked the more I heard stories of people in their own midlife turmoil. What became clear was there were distinct yet commonly blamed midlife events that transpired for nearly everyone and these events fell into seven categories. I call them **the Seven D's:**

1. **Death:** Someone you're close to dies suddenly, unexpectedly, or from disease.
2. **Divorce:** These are incredibly painful to go through. Often there's anger—lots of anger.
3. **Disease:** You receive an alarming disease diagnosis.
4. **Disillusionment:** Feelings of disillusionment and helplessness are prevalent these days as a result of political strife and social and religious divisiveness. Disillusionment also comes from uncovering unpleasant truths about people in our lives.
5. **Destruction:** When someone willfully inflicts emotional, professional, physical, mental, or legal harm or damage. (This was relevant in my case.)
6. **Dismantling:** This is a breakdown and then disappearance of a familiar structure (professional, familial) that we believed ourselves to be part of. (Also true in my case.)
7. **Devastation:** This is associated with a dramatic or hostile betrayal, a shocking situation, a singular tragic event, or a natural disaster—something that happens and is out of your control. (Yep. Been there, too.)

The commonality between people was not the "what" that had occurred, but the fact that something so big, so concrete, and so identity-shattering had happened—an event so monumental that life, and more specifically, identity, were forever altered.

Several I spoke with went through more than a single D at once, such as a family member dying while they were in the middle of divorce, or they received a disease diagnosis a week after being fired from a job. (In my case, over several years, there was Death, Divorce, Disease, Destruction, Dismantling, and Devastation.)

A fundamental attribute to share is that my D incidents thrashed me forward—suddenly and unwillingly—thrown out of a known nest and into darkness. I hate to say it, but I think it had to be that way. A bomb had to drop. The dramatic intensity of the "before" and "after" line of my identity had to be visible from space. The rip between the knowledge of my self and the Self I was to become had to be deep, permanent, and undeniable. Otherwise, I might have dabbled. I might have burrowed beneath safe sand. Who the fuck wants to be uncomfortable?

* * * * *

From Night to Flight, and Soul to Self

Speaking of comfort, notable author Brené Brown posted an article she'd written on her blog specifically about the midlife transition period. She referred to it as a midlife "unraveling." Thousands of people positively responded. It resonated with me, too. However, that term seemed quaint and I'd amend it. "Unraveling" implies that one thing gently leads to another; like a soft ball of yarn being unwound, or a stray thread that gets tugged and section by soft section, things come apart.

While my identity loss had aspects that felt like an unraveling (such as lack of control), my experience wasn't tidy. Finding a less-orderly, rougher way to describe the internal grunge and muck, mess, and uncertainty, was a step forward to call out a more accurate truth on the matter.

With the dark night of the soul as a newly understood, but not quite accurate, explanation for my identity-grief, I needed a more direct description. Why? In a nutshell, "night" seemed too neat and "soul" seemed oversimplified. Differences in word choice may seem small, but in fact they're profound to my understanding of what I went through. They became the premise of this book: midlife identity loss and the associated grief became characterized as a Dark Flight of the Self.

1) "Flight" instead of "night": The dark internal trench of my life from moment one until moment done took four years. Four long years. When I hear the word "night," it implies this thing—this transition, this plummet into the unknown—is brief and containable. The place you may be in, the place I was in, was neither.

A single night is like recalling an isolated evening of bad decisions, blurred by red solo cups filled with cheap vodka. My dissolving identity ultimately required roughly 1,417 nights to get through.

Another reason I intentionally replaced "night" with "flight": to use a metaphor describing a search for Self, it takes a long-ass time to fly across a vast ocean when you're a little bird. This transitional period of identity dismantling feels more like an exhausting flight, with no visible horizon, no discernible breeze to push you along; in fact, you may have to pump and flap against opposing wind currents, only to sputter a few feet.

Migration flights require energy and endurance to survive.

Even though some birds flock in groups, for the most part, flights are lonely and solitary.

A Dark *Flight* of the Self means straying off course with no compass, no landmarks to guide, no clue about where you're going, no idea of distance traveled. In every emotional, mental, and logistical aspect of life, you're winging it.

2) "Self" instead of "soul": For some, these words mean similar things. I believe there's a marked difference. Some people have a religious or spiritual resonance with "soul." Soul implies a core essence of who we are, separate from, and not derived out of, mental cognition. A soul is one's core being that arises—perhaps before birth—no matter what we *think* about it. A soul is one's origin spirit that is as individual as a thumbprint. Souls are believed to be infinite and to live on after bodies have perished.

Self implies a *mental awareness of who we are*, and *how we relate to who we are.* In other words, I have a mental billboard and thoughtful comprehension of my Self. I'm self-defined by established roles (woman, mother, wife, friend, etc.) which become embedded identities comprising myself. I'm invested in the relationship to these identities, which are expressions of and manifestations of my Self.

When I refer to the Dark Flight of the Self, the distinction represents **the journey of grief prompted by the changing relationship to our mental perception of who we are**. Understanding this contrast from the dark night of the soul freed me up to make room for healing. If I had known a fraction of what I now realize, the experience of identity loss might not have lasted as long. One thing's for sure: I would have been kinder to my Self. The self-blame, internal resentment and anger over my perceived inadequacy took a huge emotional toll. "What the fuck is wrong with you?" and "Why can't you get your shit together?" were daily mantras.

Generally Speaking

During the darkest parts of the transitional Flight, there was more anger directed to my Self than there was fear. That's how grief showed up. As a self-initiating person with a lifetime understanding of how I moved in the world, how I responded to situations, how I cast my mind to create reality, being in an emotional position of helplessness made me angry. But underneath the rage was something I'd never acknowledged before: I was afraid. What if I remained stuck forever? What if nothing changed?

I was afraid of dying, yet afraid of living.

I was afraid of saying too much, and afraid of not saying enough.

I was afraid of loving, but afraid of losing if I loved.

I was afraid of not being enough, yet afraid of being too much.

I was afraid of being left behind, and afraid to take the lead.

I was afraid of becoming invisible, yet afraid of being clearly seen.

I was afraid of never knowing who I really am.

I am afraid of knowing who I really am.

Being powerless to clutch onto the only tightly held Me I'd ever known as I watched my self tumble was terrifying. The sensation was like opening my mouth to scream as I dropped, only no sounds came out, while the truth of who I was rapidly fell apart. The midlife crevasse was like none before. As the descent from a previous me began and the Dark Flight took over, I floated though clouds of threatening territory.

What was so threatening?

- I'd never experienced such a sense of helplessness.
- My life was changing and I could do nothing to stop it.
- The future was uncertain.
- My past was over and never coming back.

- The only truth I'd ever counted on, a "Me" that was always there and never let me down, was formed from a house of straw.
- If I'm no longer the Me I always knew, then *who am I?*
- I didn't know where I was flying to. Or who would greet me when I was done. Or if I could ever count on Me again.

Perhaps that's what scared me the most. If I could no longer count on my Self to change what was happening, to fake it till I made it, to do and think those things that had worked in the past, then who'd be there to catch me if I crashed?

My mind was conditioned to be a beautiful bastard designed to box, name, define, and categorize. With a Dark Flight of the Self transition, I was dealing with a whole other interior realm that resisted being boxed, defined, or categorized. That was why the experience was frustrating. My practical mind couldn't understand a "who I am" that was no longer there.

One of the most deflating aspects of the Dark Flight was having no mental control. It's true that we live with an illusion of control. We can't predict outcomes of any circumstances. However, the feeling of not having any control was magnified during my Dark Flight because when I was "doing" as a way of "being," it reinforced the illusion that I had control.

By "doing," I had some control over what did and didn't happen. "Doing" emphasized the façade that my actions influenced the ripples of life's circumstances. Maybe they do, in that opportunities lead to other opportunities. A stone thrown into life's pond sets in motion waves of change.

Yet, during the Dark Flight, I didn't know what to "do." Nothing influenced internal feelings of desperation and loss. Maybe this aspect was the one that left me the most agitated. Nothing I did worked. And by "worked," I mean guided, provided insight, or created a shift in the ever-present disconnect.

I've felt helpless when people died or when it was clear there was nothing I could do to change a situation. But at the back end of change, whatever that change was, there was always Me. And I always had some action or deliberate thought as to how to get into or out of how I was feeling.

During the Dark Flight, I was shit out of luck. I was rebooting a Mac system with DOS. The software, the tools, the specific functions needed to run the system (in this case the internal system), were obsolete and incompatible. Trying to get motivated was like hitting "control-alt-delete" 72 times and having nothing happen. No matter how many times I hit the buttons, smacked the side of the computer, there was no response. Subsequent anger, pronounced impatience, with nowhere to go? Yeah, that's it.

When anger builds up and frustration has nowhere to go, one turns on one's Self. Resentment has to funnel somewhere. I certainly didn't want to take it out on my kids or my husband, so I was the obvious choice. Everything I couldn't control about what was going on became my fault.

Describing this state to others—friends, colleagues, my husband—was impossible. I couldn't convey feeling motionless, unmotivated, disconnected, and, worse, helpless to do anything to change my state. The self-blame and shame and emotional paralysis that accompanied the disconnect makes me sad.

In my former identity, I was the one to make things happen. I was the most self-initiating person I knew. This is from where irony and heart tears spring.

What happens when the person who takes charge is paralyzed?

Every day, I'd ask myself, *What the hell is wrong with me?*

Clearly, one aspect of identity that used to serve me—self-initiating into and out of motion; the Janna who had moved in the world for nearly five decades—wasn't available. It died. When the old identity dismantled so quickly, so suddenly, so completely, so, too, did all the tools and tactics that went along with it.

If you had a computer that stored everything you'd ever written and suddenly the hard drive was wiped clean without your knowledge, it would make you crazy to look for a document or file no longer there. Yet you'd go back and search the damn computer, clueless about what the hell happened to it.

Identity crash is similar. You are trying to "do" in the world in a way you've always done, when that you is no longer you. And you're still far away from the you you're going to be.

For people who "do," this disassociation sucks.

Eight years into owning a magazine, I knew that although I loved my business, I loved my work, and I loved being a publisher, my ultimate life aim was to learn how to be someone based on who I was, not based on what I did. There's a fundamental difference between being who we are based on who we are, and not based on what we do.

I know hundreds of women who function highly in their careers. I wouldn't say I hid behind my career, because I considered my career an extension of who I was in the world. My personal was professional. My professional was personal. I related to who I was through the lens of a third-person professional identity. Janna was confident. Janna could be cynical, practical, and realistic, yet she was also optimistic, hopeful, and dreamy. Janna sought solutions. Janna did her best with her business.

My career kept me from "being" because I was so busy "doing." I wondered, *What does it mean to just "be"? Who am I, separate from activity, separate from thoughts and opinions and directing busyness?* I didn't know. But I wanted to.

Why Bother?

My professional life covered the doing and thinking. I was what I produced from what I did and what I thought. This evolved because in my mind doing and thinking got shit done. Feeling and being? Not so much.

My story of how all that changed is what led me to you.

Every time I thought about getting closer, or uncovering, or peeling back the layers to a mystery Me, it made me uncomfortable. The sensation was worse than a fourth grader on the first day at a new school. Crazy, isn't it? How the thought of inching toward one's Self is inconceivable and awkward?

To understand how vulnerable the Me beneath felt to the risk of exposure, imagine an emperor stripped of every thread clothing his body, standing naked on a 10-foot-high podium in the middle of Times Square during morning rush hour.

I don't know why or how I got transported so far away from my Self. Maybe it was a mixture of childhood stuff: growing up in a single-parent home and becoming self-reliant at a way-too-early age, rationalizing that thinking instead of feeling, and doing instead of being were what saved me and kept me protected—a survival response. Once a self-reliance die was cast, I had a lifetime, literally hundreds of thousands of reinforcing moments that, similar to flowing lava, oozed from inner space, built over and buried deep in the core of an interior Self, a more innocent girl that needed emotional protection.

Perhaps it's not as essential as to how I drifted away, decade after decade, farther from Janna. How much of one's past is responsible for how we come to understand a present? I did a good job at manufacturing another Janna in her place. A hologram. As one eroded, another got built by the same Self-preservation lava. This Janna, the one I'd known forever, was the one who moved in the world, owned a business, thought about everything she saw, had responses that bypassed entire emotional land-scapes, and productively functioned.

I liked her fine enough. She'd done well and had a good life. I acknowledge that she did what she could to be self-initiating, to hold on, take responsibility, stay strong, keep everything together, protect her chil-dren, be a good wife, remain a true friend, work hard, and always have an answer for how to make things better. And when her world came crashing down and her Dark Flight began, the monumental identity shift ignited, and she had nowhere to go.

I can see how innocent the representational Janna was, too, at that time, not so unlike the Janna that had been left behind in order to survive.

Which is incredibly sad when I think about it now.

She and I were left alone.

Midlife fate initiated my Dark Flight of the Self on Wednesday, December 17, 2014. Years later, I understand that I couldn't have had a meaningful introduction to my Self until the Flight had been ignited. I wish I could deliver brighter news, but the Flight revealed that midlife identity loss had to occur. The house of straw had to burn. The Dark Flight of the Self only happens through disconnect, fear, and uncertainty. A primary way for getting closer to an unencumbered Self buried beneath that distraction is the total destruction of a superimposed self that hides it.

So why bother? This conversation became a necessity. I didn't want to go on without seeing Me through. I had a whispering feeling that some-where within was a Me that was more me, a Me that lived without a pro-fessional title, free from expectations, separate from the me I project in the world. I was worth discovering. I wanted to say hello.

I have a husband, Mark (my second marriage). We've been together nearly 10 years. The Dark Flight of the Self took a toll on our relationship. As my husband, my partner, Mark deserved to be considered throughout the process. If I was to recreate who I was in the world, this would require a form of relationship renegotiation. It's impossible for things to stay the same when everything about those things is changing. In the context of a radical midlife identity shift, I couldn't be who I was becoming in a relationship that was formed under the expectations of who I once was.

I think this is true of all relationships—with children, spouses, partners, friends, or family members. If one domino in the line-up shifts, the rest inherently follow. How we relate to our selves is in direct correlation to how we relate to others.

I have two children: my daughter, Violet, who is now 18, and my son, Ethan, who is now 14. I have incredible guilt over the span I emotionally checked out as a parent. During my Dark Flight of the Self, there were moments when I was barely hanging on. Not that I would have harmed myself or done something dramatic, but it was a fine line in terms of taking care of myself in healthy, responsive, productive ways. Could I have gone to the gym, eaten better, not smoked as much pot, drank less, taken vitamins, sucked it up? I don't know, because I didn't.

I want to let myself off the hook with what I perceive as inadequate parenting, but at the same time, this is the one area of the midlife dismantling that feels tender. I'm my own judge and jury. I'd like to be kind to myself given the circumstances, the depth of grief I felt, and the immense sense of loss. Yet I'm the first to deliver a guilty verdict.

I still functioned, getting the kids to school, picking them up, being there to help my daughter navigate a volatile late adolescence and keeping my son on track in the early days of his. But it's hard to know what grade I would have received through their transitions, because I was so out of sync with my own. More on the mommyhood topic later.

To answer the Why bother? question, I wanted to shield my children from worry as I flew through a dark time. The aim was to come out as a mother who was honest with her kids about life's emotional and developmental challenges. I wanted to be the closest version of my Self that I could be, so I could be a parent who was truly present for my children—from a place that was heart-centric, compassionate, and unfiltered.

The Dark Flight of the Self is strenuous but necessary to reach one's heart. Once one reaches one's own heart—the Self—it changes how one lives, sees, feels, gives, and connects with everyone meaningful in their life.

With my one life I have to be, do, see, become, discover, and experience, here was an opportunity to reckon how I wanted the remainder to go. Maybe midlife is *the* gift—by this stage, I'd lost friends to cancer, heart attacks, misfortune, or suicide—and I was lucky enough to have made it this far. At midlife, my cognitive ability (or wisdom) to reflect was fortified enough to make meaning of my experiences, and I still had time left to do something intentional about what came next. The risk of a deeper life was worth it. I wanted to know that I gave my Self a chance. Let me uncover, a least a little, who this woman is. I was willing to tolerate the emotional clumsiness to become familiar with a forgotten Me.

A midlife identity breakup showed me that it was time. I was making an introductory gesture of extending a hand to my Self, the one who is Me, without thinking or producing or wielding a professional title. I was extending an olive branch, making the first move, putting my other Self out there and merely looking to say hello.

Like so many others in midlife who feel lost, and lonely, and disconnected, I'd been initiated into the moment of realization: it was time to fly my way home.

Answers Are Always Questions

Many wonder what life is all about. My early pondering traces back to reading Judy Blume's *Are You There God? It's Me, Margaret.* I was 11 and remember eating that contemplative shit up. I had sprouting boobies, I lusted after Nicky Rosenberg (who didn't know I was alive), and my hormonal angst pined away on pink pages of a Hello Kitty diary. I listened to Olivia Newton-John sing *Hopelessly Devoted to You* as I died inside. What *was* it all about?

Significant transitional events—the death of a loved one, divorce, children leaving home, milestone birthdays—invoke these questions and potential feelings of helplessness, loneliness, and/or resentment. Some may ask if their life has amounted to anything or if they've made a meaningful impact.

Contemplating one's worth reminds me of a scene toward the end of the movie *Saving Private Ryan.* Matt Damon plays the character of Private Ryan, who's been saved during combat by Captain Miller, portrayed by Tom Hanks. Toward the end of the movie, Captain Miller is mortally wounded. His words to Private Ryan at the moment before his death are, "James . . . earn this. Earn it." What he means is, "Earn your gift of life that our deaths have afforded you."

Forty years later, Ryan is at Captain Miller's grave. Addressing the headstone, he whispers, "Every day I think about what you said to me that day on the bridge. And I've tried to live my life the best I could. I hope that was enough. I hope that at least in your eyes, I've earned what all of you have done for me." Later, after the graveside visit, Ryan is sitting with his wife at the kitchen table and says, "Tell me I've led a good life. Tell me I'm a good man . . ."

Ryan's struggle to define his own worth illustrates a common juncture in life, when we contemplate if we're doing all we're supposed to. Has time been wasted? Given human nature, how hard we are on ourselves, and the unrealistic expectations that society places on us on top of those we place on ourselves, even if we were as virtuous as Mother Teresa, somewhere inside we would feel as if we'd failed.

It doesn't take Hollywood drama or someone dying on our behalf to understand whether or not we've earned our life, but that moment of Ryan's questioning was genuine. While materialistic, professional, or personal desires may be complex, as humans, we want to be loved, be seen, be understood, and to belong. The question of worth is at the core of each of these. Do I matter? What am I meant to do? Who am I supposed to be? What do I have to give?

If questions lead to doubt—true, unfiltered, internal sparks of doubt—they may ignite into lightning strikes: charged, hot, and unpredictable. I have little control over the moments when I start to doubt my worth. It's hard to separate our value based on what we do from the intrinsic worth of who we are.

As an adult, I had never been alone or with my Self for an extended period of time. I'm going to share some background, which will take time to explain but drudge with me, it's part of the story. Once I moved away from home at 22, I lived alone. Throughout my 20s I never had roommates. I preferred my own space. I was by myself all the time. However, I had no desire to be with my "Self." I had no idea what that even meant. The thought of being closer to layers beneath were non-concepts, like not-yet-conceived children.

My concerns focused on making money to pay bills, going out with friends, partying, and giving attention to whatever things/circumstances/people were in front of me. Which is fine. I did what I was supposed to do and be in my 20s.

I met my first husband, Billy, the father of my children, a few weeks after I turned 30. A succession of events over the next three years as we began our life together led to a reverse order of pregnancy and then marriage (which we'd already planned as eventual probability), and toward the circumstances that followed over the next 20 years.

I got married in March of 2000. That August, at 33 years old, I gave birth to my daughter, Violet. Four years later, at 37, I had my son, Ethan. Probably not the oldest mother that ever lived, but not a spring chicken in the realm of child bearing, either.

Also in 2004, I purchased my business, *Local Living* magazine, an endeavor that for the next decade required a metric ton of dedication as well as relentless headaches and heartaches, especially to keep it afloat during the economic meltdown of 2009.

More detail about these life-shifting events later, but the point is that by the time the urge kicked in to get a smidgen closer to what lurked internally—somewhere around age 43 or 44—I no longer had any capacity. I was a hamster on an automated wheel, spinning around and around and around trying to keep up. Something was missing. I didn't know what the empty feelings were, and I couldn't name them. My life was a blur of stuff.

So many details and expectations and things to get done and children to raise and a business to run. I churned within a vicious cycle of daily expectations/shit to get done/shit to think about/new shit to get done, and on and on.

There's an illusion here, a big one, that we always have things to take care of. Every waking second of existence we fill our lives and heads and schedules with thousands of details to attend to, manage, sort, judge, name, blame, shift, deny, pack, stack, build, and (rarely) ignore.

I'm not saying that as women, mothers, wives, friends, employees, or business owners we don't have things to attend to. We have to manage a life based on whatever existence we have. I don't want to take away from the life I've built; I'm aware there are places on Earth where life for women is very different—places where daily matters revolve around survival: walking miles to fetch drinkable water; milking a goat to feed children; hiding any form of opinion because otherwise, just being alive as a woman becomes risky.

We are who we are. In this conversation, I'm speaking about most women I know who have built a life around a sundry of social expectations, norms, and mores. We. Are. Production. Machines. Do. Do. Do.

Around my mid-40s, I remember a yearning to know more about who I was based on how I *felt*, not on what I *thought;* I wanted to explore who I was based on how I was *being* in the world and not on what I *did* for a living.

As its publisher, *Local Living* magazine was my identity. My business was personal. And my personhood was my business. I was who I was because of *Local Living.* And *Local Living* was the magazine it was because of me. We—our identities, existences, realities—were inextricably intertwined.

Being a publisher was how I got invitations to community events and complimentary tickets to concerts, theater, and exhibits. It was the cloak that inspired notable community leaders to cozy up. The title yielded invitations for fabulous press trips to places like Maui and Fiji. Since the publication was geared toward families, I brought my kids along on a lot of fun adventures.

I never took these opportunities for granted. I sent thank-you cards to anyone who extended a hand. I was in a fortunate position and made efforts to share the wealth. I passed along comp tickets for concerts to friends or those who worked for me. I felt strongly about distributing the perks that came with owning this type of business.

Many aspects of this work, this specific business, this medium, were fundamental to my nature; seeking and sharing meaningful stories of people, places, and ideas to inspire human understanding and connection. Owning a magazine was mission driven.

Every month, I had pages to fill with stories that brought to life the heart of people's experiences. Interestingly, by focusing on what was "out there" month after month, gathering ideas amidst the landscape of stuff about other people's lives, then distilling, editing, and assigning imagery to them, I completely bypassed my Self.

I was always surveying the outside, hovering and observing the exterior world. Scanning thousands of pieces of information for the timely and timeless: relevant, publication-worthy content. And all this within a clockwork schedule of daily, weekly, and monthly deadlines. I got good at recognizing the heart of *other* people's stories. By always looking out I never had time to look in.

My functionality and productivity in my work kept me from Me.

Let's add another layer. Aside from the creative/editorial component of producing a magazine—the skill required to make a monthly magazine content rich—there were operational logistics to ensure I could pay people who designed, distributed, and printed the magazine. I was the only one bringing in revenue. Magazines depend upon advertisers. Advertisers pay for ads, ads pay for the printing, content, and distribution. In theory, ad revenue should have also covered my salary. Some months it did, and many months it didn't.

To get businesses to advertise took relationship investment, conversation and consistency. I had to ensure existing advertisers were happy as well as pound the pavement to drum up new clients. This entailed cold-calling businesses that seemed like a good fit, finding the right person to speak with, getting them interested in meeting, setting up appointments, going to the appointments, then following up with lengthy proposals based on what was discussed, until deals were done.

I enjoyed meeting new people and loved learning about how their businesses served the community. The connections were the best part of my job. I believed in the mission of the magazine (keeping families educated and inspired) and the authenticity of the stories *Local Living* presented. I never felt like I was engaged in sales, even though that's what it was.

I didn't view the connections I had to make as work, per se, although I was aware that the lifeblood of the magazine was a steady stream of monthly revenues. Meeting a high financial quota month after month was a lot of pressure.

Although I was my own boss and could technically come and go as I pleased, I was always "on." I was never *not* thinking about the magazine or some thing (usually many things) that needed to be done. If I went on a press trip to Maui, I was working. This meant I had a schedule or itinerary to follow: public relations people to meet, editorial obligations to fulfill, a story to write about my experience.

I don't mean to sound like a prima donna. *Wow, she had to work while she's getting a paid trip to Maui!* But it's important to acknowledge impacts and that more than one truth can exist at the same time. No matter where I was, what I was doing, who I was with, I felt mentally obligated to the job. I was never free. Not for a minute. And even while on those beautiful press trips, looking at the ocean, I had a hard time being in the moment because I was always thinking about the people that needed to be called, articles that needed writing and editing, graphic layouts to consider, or the huge avalanche of bills that I, as owner, was ultimately responsible for each month. I felt conflicted.

Every hour of every day, each day of every week, there was a long list of unforgiving financial and editorial deadlines. I was still running the wheel whether I was sick, on Maui, tired, or felt like running away. Whether it was 6 a.m. on a Saturday, friends were visiting from out of town, or I needed to attend my grandmother's funeral. I was trapped in managing the outcome of something.

I share this background to highlight how conditioned I became to "doing." My mind was *always* clicking. Everything I did had an expected result. And that result better be productive.

None of the mind-exploding, externally driven world of expectations even factored in the rest of my life. My first husband, Billy, wasn't much of an emotional or financial factor at home throughout periods of our marriage. He was a budding unconfident artist trying to build a career, but he had none of the self-confidence skills required for business success as an artist. He was introverted and didn't promote himself or his art. The household income burden was on me. I had two kids to raise and was the primary breadwinner.

The ways we parented, disciplined, and supported our children were different, too. I wanted to provide my kids with as much external enrichment as possible. I had no problem spending money on things I considered needed for their growth such as a good education, summer camps, or classes based on art or recreation. Billy usually didn't agree. Our values on money varied as well. I hold no resentment or bitterness. As a mother, I did what I thought was best for them. These are merely facts being presented.

Emotionally I felt alone, too. It may be accurate to say that because of our fundamental personality differences, I was independent from the marriage. Being on my own, making decisions for myself and my kids, taking care of the bills and structure and daily details of life, I felt the weight and expectations of everything and everyone all the time.

There were times I'd be dressed to go to a meeting, carrying a computer case over my shoulder and heading for the door, and Violet would come running after me, crying for me not to leave. "Maawwwmmmy!!!" she'd wail. She'd put up her little four-year-old arms, reaching for me with twinkling little fingers, giant tears coming out of her big blue eyes, and my heart would shatter. Sometimes she'd cling to my leg, other times she'd just plop where she was in defeat, and I'd feel like total shit. I'd be crying in the driveway, watching Violet's round face stare at me as I drove away. I would arrive at my appointments with mascara streaks beneath my eyes and a red nose.

This ever-present guilt from the competing requirements of motherhood and keeping my business and house alive, the burden of having to be both, do both, and not let the other fall apart, accompanied me the entire 10 years I owned the magazine. I worked from home, but I was never really there.

The scars on the magazine would be immediate if I faltered. But the scars on my kids—who wanted me to play with them, read to them, color with them, and were met with my irritation because I was trying to get stuff done—well, that's for a future psychiatrist's couch to reveal.

Billy and I spent our last year together in counseling to see what we could repair. Ultimately, after 13 years of being together, 10 of them married, he found his exit. While I thought we were doing what we could to save things (even though I could sense an end), he had spent months entangled with the person he's still with today.

My kids may read this someday, and I want them to know that I'm not sorry about the way things turned out. Their father is happy; I'm happy. I'm looking at this through the eyes of an adult, so I understand the way the marriage crashed was dramatic for them. I will never know Billy's story. I understand he did what he thought he had to do. However, I wish the marriage's end could have been handled differently. But hey, I got two of my life's greatest treasures out of the deal. Not a single regret.

This backstory relates to the big picture because all the pieces of my professional life and first marriage fit into the groundwork for how I came to be and why I fell so hard into darkness. I was shouldering emotional and mental responsibility in every corner of my life. I could observe who I was—but had no real connection to who I was. Everything I was came from what I did, thought, or produced.

From my mid-40s on, the whisper of "Who am I?" remained, nagging. I can't label it as dissatisfaction. I never felt like I wanted another life. I was stressed out, a lot, but that didn't catch up to me until a few years later. The whisper was more about who I would be if not for what I did?

Here Are Two Stories...

This first section of this book, "Me," is about how I formed a basis of who I believed I was in the world. The circumstantial pieces of my life—the weight of what I did for a living and the role I publicly played, a crumbling marriage of choreographed logistics, plus a devastating loss of my beloved grandma—formed the identity castle I'd come to live in. The circumstances created a level of grief that, up to that point, I'd not experienced.

I'm sharing two stories here to illustrate the period of loss that occurred from my early to mid-40s. Both are Ds—Death and Divorce— and they set into motion a heightened awareness about loss and grief.

I believe that a midlife Dark Flight of the Self includes a deeper awareness of death as inevitable. With the first story, by going through my grandma's passing alongside her, I experienced a loss of innocence. When she died so did a part of my sacred childhood and thus, a part of my identity.

STORY #1:

Mourning of Innocence

November 1, 2009. All Saints Day. Día de los Muertos. The day my grandmother Freda took her last breath. She was 96.

My grandmother was a vivacious, loving, independent woman. Until her third stroke in her late 80s, she got up every morning before 7 a.m., put on a brightly colored sweater with perfectly matched clip-on earrings, and walked five miles roundtrip to Canter's for a bagel and "cawfee" as her faint Jersey accent pronounced it. She didn't miss a day. For as long as I recall, no matter life's hiccups—death of my grandpa, death of her two sisters, death of her friends—she got up and greeted her day.

I admired this wake-up-and-do-what-you-got-to-do in her. I'm not sure if it was self-love or self-discipline. I'd love to ask her.

Seeing her physically change over a five-year period after a succession of strokes was difficult. After the first two, which were a couple of months apart, she remarkably bounced back. Though paralyzed on one side and having been told by doctors she'd never walk again, after six weeks of physical therapy, she was shuffling along with the aid of a walker. She could still speak, though her words were slurred. Having diminished capacity must have been hard for her, but she kept going.

By then, my mom had been living with her for a few years. When my grandma's ability to live independently vanished—more as a result of mental than physical faltering (stoves left on, doors left unlocked)—my mom made the sacrifice to move in with her. Eventually, however, the succession of strokes also required a live-in caregiver.

My mom would go through the process of interviewing, hiring, then justifiably firing a revolving door of caregivers. Some would stay a few weeks, others a few months. Over those years, there were a couple of good ones. People who actually showed up and did what was supposed to be done: care for my grandma. At minimum, she needed to be bathed, dressed, and fed; a bonus was to be shown compassion and love. I felt the constant quandary my mom was in, having to locate an angel.

Then Charme showed up. She'd be the last caregiver my grandma had until she died. Charme was with our family for a couple of years. I was grateful for the love, kindness, and humanity she offered to a grandmother I struggled to recognize. After all the goodness my grandma had shared in her life, she deserved the same at the end of hers.

I wished Charme could have known my grandma as she'd been before her strokes, not the version that was unable-to-speak-and-barely-able-to-walk. Charme loved my grandma anyway. Charme would have appreciated the independent, always laughing, sharp-as-a-tack Freda.

On October 22, 2009, my grandma had her final stroke. It was a doozy. I got the call that I should fly home to Los Angeles. I brought my daughter Violet, who was then nine years old. We went straight from the airport to the hospital. My grandma was lifeless in a bed, hooked up to a labyrinth of machines. There would be no miracles. No bouncing back. My heart broke as I held her soft hand.

I'd never been in front of death. Lysol smell, beeping wires, and other people's collective sadness were terrifying. After a couple of strange days, a decision was made for wires and feeding tubes to be removed. My grandma would die at home. We tidied up details to make the unbearable tangible. I figured without food, water, or life support, my grandma might make it another few days.

Once she was home, though, the days and nights dragged. I speculated as to why my grandma was hanging on. Was there unfinished business? Was she in limbo and like the strong, unyielding person she was in life, was she avoiding death? Was she entangled in some physical/spiritual snare?

I felt helpless. After six days of sitting on my hands waiting for death, I called a recommended spiritual medium to come over and help her break free, in the far-off chance her soul was in limbo. As out-there as it seemed, I would have done anything to relieve her suffering as I watched her restless body struggle. Charles the medium sat with my mother and I at my grandma's white, oval-shaped kitchen table and began to recite eerily accurate insights about her life, her hopes for us, and a few of her regrets. He said she joked about not having the right earrings for the nightgown we'd dressed her in.

After an hour and dozens of words, Charles created a passage-assistance ritual. He went into a trancelike state, softly chanting and waving a partially dried limb of burning cedar. With his eyes closed, the chanting got louder and at the precise moment he finished (I kid you not) an inexplicably huge gust of wind whipped through the yard outside and through the kitchen in the house, even though the windows were closed. I heard the slam of metal garbage cans from the driveway that had been tossed in the air.

As if nothing extraordinary had just occurred and without skipping a beat, Charles the medium assured us he had cleared my grandma's remaining earthly tethers, and it wouldn't be long. After he left, I was unsettled by the thunderous gust-burst from an otherwise windless day and I felt *something*. I'm not sure relief is the right word. But I no longer wanted to watch her waiting, struggling for breath. There was comfort in hoping all was aligned in her spirt and heart and she'd soon be free.

The next night was Halloween. It was a nearly full, waning moon. For those who grow up or live in Los Angeles it's known that Halloween in West Hollywood is that little city's biggest night of the year. My grandmother lived in the heart of West Hollywood. Both waiting for and dreading her end, I decided to take a drive.

As I meandered the West Hollywood streets, I melted within the carnival freak show. Ghosts, and skeletons, and vampires, and huge, pink feather boas, and drag queens, and sailors, and zombies, and people partying and drinking and busting out at the seams of the streets—they all laughed and caroused while my grandmother's death was palpable. No matter which corner I turned or which street light I stopped at, I couldn't escape. I could feel my grandmother's constricted breath with mine.

Exaggerated snapshots of aliveness taunted me; debauchery and unapologetic costumed expressions of the veil between light and dark got neatly wrapped into a parade of pink boa feathers. And with it, so did my innocence.

November 1, I wanted to get Violet out of the house for a while. She'd been a trouper. I took her around the corner for breakfast to a place called Norm's. Halfway through the pancakes, I got the call.

My mom and brother had been with her. It was a Sunday.

* * * * *

This second story, "Keys to Oneself," I wrote towards the end of my marriage to Billy nine months after my grandma died. When I see this story now I recall how lost I was behind the external stuff of my life. Even then, there were definite whispers from a deeper Me that wanted *me* to search and find her. The poem was poignant and every time I read it, still, nearly 10 years later, I'm grateful for a stranger's everlasting words.

STORY # 2

Keys to Oneself - August, 2010

Walking in downtown Portland is an excursion. Especially on a sunbaked day. I had much on my mind about my dissipating marriage to Billy as I shuffled along. The cement gleamed. People hustled. Petitioners vied for signatures. With an extra 30 minutes until my next business meeting, I headed toward Macy's to explore earrings. Yep—that would help me feel better. Shiny, sparkly earrings.

On the corner of Broadway and Morrison, I noticed a man sitting within a makeshift station consisting of a chair, TV tray, and small type-writer. His sign dangled from the tray, and written in black Sharpie on a box top were the words, "Poems for You."

I needed meaningful words. Instead of sparkly earrings, I needed serendipitous reassurance that someday, maybe even today, my world would once again be alright. His name was Bill. His offering (by dona-tion) was while-you-wait street poetry. I fell in love with the Portlandness of this: a makeshift station, a literary artist, tapping on-the-fly words upon the keys of a tiny antique typewriter, based on a subject of the recipient's request. I handed him $10.

"What would you like your poem to be about?" asked Bill.

"Hmm," I vacillated. "How about finding one's Self?"

"Ah . . . the proverbial search for self. The journey of what has to be lost in order to be gained . . ."

I stood beside him as he typed, tapped, and spun the ribbon spool around a few times to release the tangles. Click-click-click-clack-clack-click-click-clack the keys danced in rhythm toward my fortune.

When done, he yanked the paper through the carriage. Bill held "Finding Oneself" in front of us as he recited his magical creation:

```
FINDING ONESELF, By Bill Keys
I would suppose that the first step in any search
is a description of the lost
and so clues as to where and when and what
I've looked in the mirror
     seems an obvious start
but the guy in the glass was a convincing fake
my lover was convinced that it wasn't me she slept with
but a much more productive chap
someone who likes yoga
I asked my mom and she said I was as good as it gets
that I was someone destined for the big lights
Alone I ache filled with a hole filled with echoes
Alone in the anxious demand of the air
to fill the wide-open field inside
perhaps flowers
        maybe corn wheat?
Alone my racing mind gets as tired as any Olympian
and falls quiet
     just a sweet breeze
```

```
fragrant night air
   full of dreaming
   and peace is
a silent eye
   seeing all
      seeing me
```

His words flowed and so did my repressed tears. The poem was beautiful.

I loved the randomness of the moment and the warm summer sun, the bustle of a street corner as people walked by, and a renewed sense that hope is sometimes only a few typewriter keys away.

Arrival of My D-Day

Here's where I review the succession of circumstances that led up to the distinct moments when my identity shattered—the arrival of a few more D's—to ignite my Dark Flight of the Self. I'll ask for patience as details are sorted out.

Before owning *Local Living* magazine from 2004 to 2014, I was self-employed as a public relations consultant to many nonprofits and small businesses in Portland, Oregon. Eventually, long-term financial security became a question. I was in my late 30s, had two small children, and was the primary breadwinner of my family as my then husband helped out with kids and sought to build an art business. Because I was self-employed, if something happened to me—I got injured, or died—my children would be left with nothing.

As a PR consultant, my job was to recognize and then pitch media-worthy stories waiting to be unearthed from the nonprofits I served. I worked with some of Portland's greatest organizations, including Outside In (housing, education, job placement, and medical services for homeless youth); Cascade AIDS Project (advocacy, housing, and support for those affected by HIV or AIDS); and House of Umoja (a residential program for former African-American gang youth).

I was honored to learn about the positive efforts of those on the front lines making a difference, and I was able to recognize specific programs, or volunteers, or clients that the media would be interested in covering. Those working at the nonprofits, doing what they did each day, had a hard time seeing their work as newsworthy.

I made a decent living doing PR consulting. I had about five or six clients at any given time. Some short-term, maybe a few months here or there. Others, like Outside In and Cascade AIDS Project, I worked with for years. I was known for having a passion for nonprofit growth and donor development through increased public awareness.

A second part of public relations work was to present stories to reporters. I had established connections with people from radio, television, and print. I had a knack for understanding who, from which outlet, wanted which types of stories. The world of public relations is a big piece of paper with two columns: story ideas in one column, media people in the other. I was efficient at matching the two.

Twenty years ago, media held more prominence. Most news and media companies had healthy rosters of journalists covering a myriad of topics. Each outlet had its own place and purpose in terms of the type of coverage provided. I saved journalists time and offered content ideas. And yes, I used the phone a lot and preferred voice-to-voice communication over email. I sent birthdays cards and thank-you notes. The connections were personal.

I believed media companies had a social obligation to serve the public with meaningful information. I didn't appreciate how, over the years, media—including news, television programming, print products, and movies—had increasingly broadcast content that was sensationalized, sexualized, or violent. (Social media was not yet a factor in information dissemination. Can you remember existence before social media?)

Media shapes how we view and interact with the world. There are countless ways to measure negative social impacts wrought by a current broadcast ethos of sex, violence, and consumerism. I felt then and still do today that there's a necessity to offer positive stories within the sea of sludge. This ties into my story—realizing a shift was needed from being a consultant, to having an entity outside myself to create a backup financial funnel. I also still had a passion for the importance of positive stories— and I knew a lot of media people.

One of my contacts included Laura, the publisher of *Local Living* magazine, which at that time was a newsprint tabloid and had been around for 10 years. There were two family publications in the market: *Local Living* and *Portland Parent*. They were different from one another. People often read both. As was typical of family publications of that era, they both catered to a demographic of families with younger children.

These publications were useful for calendars of things to do with kids (the online calendar thing wasn't a thing yet) and had generic articles that every other free regional family magazine of that era published. Advertisements came from camps, classes, schools, and special events geared toward young kids.

In the spring of 2004, I had a conversation with Laura. She knew I had many contacts in the media business and asked me to keep my eyes open for someone who might want to purchase *Local Living*. I responded with follow-up questions related to the asking price and her desired timing of the sale. Within a few days, a lightbulb flipped on in my head. Why not me? Professionally, given my editorial and relationship-building expertise, this type of business made sense. Graphically and editorially, the magazine as it was then was . . . well, there was room for improvement.

The cost of the publication was more than $100,000 and less than $300,000. I had about $10,000 in savings and for some reason, the thought of acquiring thousands more didn't seem insurmountable. Back then I was invincible. "No," or failure, were not options. I had a trifecta of confidence, optimism, and self-reliance. If there were dreams or opportunities, I'd make them mine. This way of looking at the world and myself didn't derive from arrogance. It had to do with a fundamental belief that we individually make or break what happens in our lives. That we're ultimately responsible for what does or doesn't occur. That everything we see, feel, hear, or think solely rests upon our abilities to create them.

I investigated the financial components of a business loan. I went to the local Small Business Administration office and met with an advisor to discuss what was needed to secure a loan. I was provided a list of guidelines for a business plan. I spent the next week preparing the plan and the following week met with several banks to get a loan. I got turned down by two, but at the third bank, a nice guy named Doug from U.S. Bank spent a great deal of time working with me and advocating on my behalf to get the loan.

After U.S. Bank reviewed my plan, they agreed to give me the loan on the stipulation that my house went in as collateral and I had to come up with $40,000 cash. These stipulations were not seen, felt, or experienced as obstacles. I need $40,000 by next week? Sure, no problem.

In November of that year, miracle of miracles (after knocking on friends' and family's doors, selling some things, and kicking in the $10,000 I'd saved), I raised the $40,000. I put the deed to my house on the loan, signed documents, and bought a magazine.

I was 37 years old and it was an exciting time. I had given birth to my son, Ethan, in July. My daughter Violet was four. I became a publisher of a magazine. I had a business, an important title, a purpose, and the next big chapter of my life was beginning.

Although I knew some aspects of the business, the systems I inherited from Laura were archaic. I had to wade my way through a lot of mud that first year, without the advantage of anyone familiar with this business model to help, which meant I had to learn about everything. Magazines are very specific. Primary facets include editorial strategy, distribution models, design and production, operations, and revenue generation. There are endless logistics. I amassed an encyclopedic knowledge of magazine publishing; if anyone ever needed to hire someone to create or run a custom publication (which is part of what I do for work now), I'm the gal to call.

The realities of magazine ownership, both challenging and amazing, started to come forward in the first six months and would remain true over the next decade. For instance, I bought the publication in November and the next February, when it was cold, wet, and dreary, the Maui Visitor's Bureau came to town for a press junket. As a publisher, I'd been invited to a lunch they hosted for media. I'll never forget that day.

Aside from staff and a cultural advisor from the Maui Visitor's Bureau, there were a dozen people representing hotels, resorts, spas, and attractions. (I later coined these lunches as "lei and poi shows.") The Maui Visitor's Bureau was adept at pulling out the aloha magic of their island to entice us.

In addition to a spread of gorgeous Hawai'ian food prepared by one of Maui's best chefs, they crafted a lovely cultural ceremony. Sweet-smelling leis were placed on each guest as we arrived and during the meal they strummed ukuleles, sang seductive chants, and gracefully danced hula. I was mesmerized.

By the end of the meal, I'd met with representatives from the Hyatt, the Westin, a few luau companies, a sailboat excursion company, and a couple of spas. As a family-centric publication, *Local Living* was on target. Family travel to Maui from the Northwest was an important tourism demographic. I'd received business cards and was promised a mostly all-expenses-paid trip to Maui which included airfare, car rental, hotels, and meals. Seeds were planted that there were perks from owning this type of business. Over the 10 ownership years, there were months I couldn't pay myself because the business struggled, but I could count on some incredible experiences.

I did go to Maui that May with my daughter, who was then five. Maui Visitor's Bureau took care of me. My itinerary was full with delicious meals, fantastic excursions, and cultural experiences. In turn, I wrote about everything we saw, felt, tasted, and discovered, imparting the importance of creating beautiful memories together as a family by way of shared cultural experiences.

I believed then and still do today that meaningful stories have the power to heal, transform, inspire, educate, and open up a world of possibility. It is a responsibility and honor to be a custodian of people's stories. As such, I never took opportunities for granted and worked to maintain content integrity. In the editorial world, I developed a reputation for doing deeper, more personally nuanced profile pieces. I got to meet, interview, and write stories about many amazing people, including New York Times columnist Nicholas Kristof, Portland Trailblazer president Larry Miller, Everclear singer and guitarist Art Alexakis, founder of Dave's Killer Bread Dave Dahl, Ben Cohen of Ben & Jerry's ice cream, famed artist Peter Max, iconic singer Linda Ronstadt, film director Gus Van Sant, and so many others who lived in or visited Portland.

Everything that went into the magazine, page after page, issue after issue, was carefully considered. I covered a range of topics about education, recreation, travel, health, technology, and community. "Family" as an editorial guidepost was inclusive of many configurations and definitions. Each month, thousands of readers looked forward to reading *Local Living*.

In turn, I received tremendous satisfaction knowing I was making a small difference in the media landscape. I loved getting letters and emails from people saying that a story I wrote inspired them or opened up a door in their life. Connection through words made me happy.

Relationships with advertisers were based on a similar desire to create beneficial opportunities. I enjoyed the marketing people I worked with who made budget decisions and supported *Local Living* through advertisements, including Krista from the Oregon Zoo, Reid from Saturday Market, and Marty from Oregon Episcopal School.

These people became trusted colleagues. I was grateful for their loyalty when they had many choices for spending marketing dollars. The symbiotic relationships took years to cultivate. I had relationships and revenue to keep up with, editorial decisions to make, logistics to manage, and distribution adjustments to make, all while keeping an eye on how the magazine could eventually grow. Publication survival is all about strategy.

I loved *Local Living*. The care and attention devoted to it were extensions of me; of how I felt about the world. I was very much part of the magazine. And the magazine was part of me.

* * * * *

Nine years into *Local Living* magazine ownership, two things became evident. One, I'd taken the publication as far as I could with limited resources. It needed a cash infusion to expand beyond its capacity, through video, a stronger online presence, events, and other multimedia forms of communication. Industry changes required it.

The second thing was that I was always stressed. The monthly publication schedule was a grind that never let up. In all those years, I never had a real break, mental or otherwise. The pressure to generate revenue, create, and perform were always with me, 24 hours a day. Seeing the challenges, I started to think about selling the publication.

I went to SCORE (Service Corps of Retired Executives), a nonprofit that provides "free business mentoring services to prospective and established small business owners." I sought help to create an impartial valuation of *Local Living's* worth. I was paired with a retired publisher. We spent three months going over financial revenue, tax statements, projected receivables, annual contracts, and other intangible aspects that held value. I received a spreadsheet of what the company was believed to be worth using several different formulas.

The amount wasn't millions of dollars more than I paid, but in nine years, *Local Living* had substantially grown in worth. Eight years into ownership, I'd paid back the entire business loan. I was incredibly proud of that fact and happy to no longer have a monthly $2,200 business loan payment to worry about. I knew how hard I'd worked. I had grown to become a very skilled publisher. Business sale proceeds were going toward retirement and college funds for my kids. I'd spent a decade building a small but tangible nest egg. Once I had the value of the company, I explored selling it.

While I was publisher of *Local Living*, out of personal financial necessity, I maintained several marketing clients. Sometimes clients would refer others to me because they were happy with work I'd done for them. In the spring of 2013, I received one such call. A gentleman, Bob, from a company named Healthline, phoned to inquire about my marketing consultation services. Healthline was a new, still-in-design online portal created to connect healthcare providers with people searching for those services. It was to be a web source within a Yelp-like sphere geared toward health.

Bob had been referred by a woman named Terry. Terry owned a local spa—I'd reached out to her as a potential *Local Living* advertiser. I'd called her several times because I believed *Local Living* was an ideal fit for her business. Over the years, Terry had never returned my calls, but because she appreciated the unique way I had approached her, she thought to pass along my name to Bob.

Bob and I talked over Healthline's marketing needs, who they aimed to reach, ideas for branding. I had confidence I could help and proposed a four-month contract which included creating a branding concept, a tagline, and marketing strategy. I outlined what I would do, when I would do it, how it would get done. They hired me.

A few months into our work and delivery of what had been outlined, Bob felt the project scope required a deeper dive. He said it would be in the best interest of Healthline to introduce me to Terry, who was a Healthline shareholder. My first face-to-face meeting with Terry was in May 2013. Terry and I talked about the way she wanted to grow her company, and how she wanted to reach women. I knew that market; I'd spent the past nine years serving it.

Terry was a wealthy woman nearing 60. She had bags o' money from a huge divorce settlement. Her palatial house was located in an expensive zip code. Terry had a band of six minions who worked for her and Healthline.

When I first met Terry, she was strange and reserved but I liked her. She and I had many conversations about business, about growing Healthline, about the importance of connection through media. Over the fall and into winter, I'd completed the Healthline contract. By then I'd shared many ideas about marketing to women.

One day after we talked, it hit me: perhaps Terry would be the ideal person to buy *Local Living*. She had the financial means, she'd run businesses before, and Healthline would ideally pair with my print publication. With planning and strategy, each of us could help the other grow. *Local Living* had an established audience. She'd have access to a built-in advertising mechanism to expand her online entity. The missions of supporting health, family, and women aligned.

I invited Terry to lunch. I shared the initial sale/merge concept and the company's worth to gauge her response. She was interested. Over the next few months, I provided tax statements, the valuation from SCORE, and other supporting documentation that revealed a detailed snapshot of the company's viability. Terry was a former CFO of a large company, with extensive accounting knowledge. If there were any financial red flags, she had the credentials to spot them.

Without prompting alarm for those working with me in case the deal didn't go through, due diligence was conducted on the quiet side. I had two people, Helga and Jay, who had worked for *Local Living* for nearly the entire decade.

Helga had been a driver, delivering magazines, when I bought the company from Laura. Helga reminded me of Shleprock—things around her always fell apart. She was a stream of emotional, physical, and logistical problems. Every day it was something.

Over the years, Helga's duties increased with *Local Living*. This was partly because I felt sorry for her and partly because she seemed dedicated to the magazine. Toward the end of our 10-year run, Helga was in charge of keeping the books, doing the invoicing, and managing distribution.

Even when times got tough around years six and seven (and they got really, really tough during the economic downturn—to a point where the magazine was on life support for a few months, but managed to pull through and later thrive) Helga stuck it out. But what I needed Helga to accomplish—her job responsibilities around keeping things running—didn't get done on a frequent basis. Sometimes they did, but often not. I was spread thin and couldn't take on her responsibilities as well as mine. Yet for what I perceived as her loyalty, I was grateful, and I resisted firing her. This unhealthy back and forth between feeling sorry for her and not wanting to fire her, but being impacted by her inconsistent job performance, went on for years. I should have let her go, and my terrible business decision was to keep her—a decision that later proved fateful.

Jay was the magazine's graphic designer. She did a good job and overall, we had a decent working relationship.

During the economic downturn, for about six months, things sucked. There were months I couldn't pay people. I couldn't pay the printer, I couldn't pay Helga or Jay, I couldn't pay writers, and I definitely never paid myself. A huge chunk of advertiser money dried up. I was several months behind on bills. Many advertisers went out of business and still owed thousands of dollars to *Local Living* for placed ads. The magazine supported many smaller businesses that didn't have the bandwidth to survive the crash. Companies pulled back on spending and advertising expenses were the first to go.

I tried to be as honest as I could with Helga and Jay. I hoped transparency and proven past business performance would be considered. I thought loyalty counted for something, but there were a lot of justifiably frustrated people. Anyone on the outside would never understand the hard choices, difficulties, guilt, or sense of responsibility a business owner faces when they are alone with a bucket, bailing water out of a leaky ship.

During this time, I felt a huge sense of loss and failure, even though the economic meltdown wasn't my fault. I evaluated what I would do. I'd worked hard for years to build the business. It seemed too early to let *Local Living* go. She still had breath and she still had life. I was not willing to cut the cord.

I recommitted myself to the *Local Living* cause, and for the next three years worked hard to make the ship seaworthy again. Slowly, bills were paid, cash from advertisers flowed back in, and things picked up in the economy. I paid back every dime to every business or person owed money. The magazine had a stretch of true vitality and strength, with 3 years of solid, increased profits. It was in excellent shape when I approached Terry about purchasing it.

In December 2013, Terry informed me she wanted to purchase *Local Living*. She agreed to the asking price, but she wanted to divide the purchase into three payments—one up-front, one before December 31, 2014, and the last installment to be spread out over 12 months—if I'd agree to stay on for at least a year to help her get up to speed in the publishing world.

In March 2014, documents were crafted by her lawyers. Since we had discussed for months how this would unfold and the terms appeared simple and straightforward, I didn't retain a lawyer. I trusted Terry. We seemed to be on the same page. I agreed to her financial terms because I had no intention of going anywhere. I would never abandon *Local Living*, and if that's what she needed for assurance, I was okay with that. I agreed to stay with *Local Living* for a year as an employee because I was willing to do whatever was needed to ensure the company and Terry succeeded.

In retrospect, I see now that not having a lawyer for the sale of the magazine was one of the dumbest businesses decisions I've ever made (after not firing Helga). But considering where my heart and mind and loyalty to the publication were at that time, I was recklessly naive. In theory, everything was perfect: I trusted Terry; she had financial bandwidth to invest and take the company to a new level; I was thrilled *Local Living* would receive the infusion it deserved to bring about the next amazing chapter.

I had the chance to reflect on what an amazing publishing run it had been, all the ways I'd grown the magazine in terms of reputation, editorial quality, visual beauty, advertising partnerships, multimedia capacity, revenue sustainability, and social impact. Both personally and professionally, I had much to be proud of and wanted the best for everyone—for Terry to grow the online health company; for the magazine into which I'd poured blood, sweat, and tears to exceed what I could do for it; and for the shekels I'd received in the sale to be put away into college funds for my kids and a retirement fund for me. I had a year to plan for the next incarnation of me. I'd only had *Local Living* for a decade. What, or more specifically, who, would I be without it?

It was a beautiful picture.

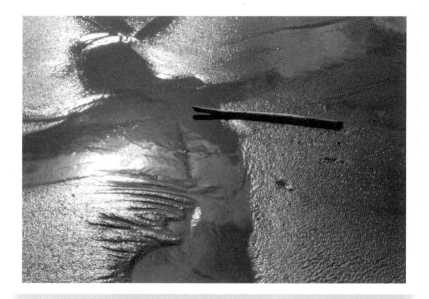

We're Done.

June 2014.

I began making calls to colleagues and friends with the news. July 1 was the official transfer of ownership to Terry. Because people knew how much I loved *Local Living*, they were shocked I was selling it. The aim was to spend June getting to know her minions and introducing Terry to some of *Local Living*'s bigger advertisers.

A few days before the end of June was signing day at Terry's attorney's office. I wore a tiara and brought a dozen roses. I was nervous and giddy and sad and hopeful about all the changes ahead. After I signed a few pages, I took off the tiara, gave it to Terry and handed her the roses. I have a photo of that moment that crushes me when I look at it now.

There was still an innocence in my eyes. I had hope for the future. For *Local Living*. I never could have imagined what was going to transpire after that day.

Over the next several months, many gigantic, bright red flags were waved; I embarrassingly admit now how naive I was. Prior to the sale, Terry had asked about Helga and Jay. Because I knew Terry would have a ramp-up phase of learning the business and because when I'd bought the company, I'd been left high and dry as far as insight or training from the prior owner, I pledged to be as helpful as possible.

Jay could carry out her designer role. She was reliable and knew the print production that kept *Local Living* running smoothly. However, I had tremendous reservations about Helga. Based on years of unreliability, Helga was a hindrance, not a help. Because Terry had an accounting background, I didn't worry about the bookkeeping aspects of the operation. However, Helga had a hold on the distribution. She knew how, where, and when the magazine got distributed each month. Disruption in this regard could have a significant impact. I shared what I felt were the pros and cons about Helga. I recommended that Helga stay only until Terry decided she wanted to do something different about distribution.

The next area to sort out was sales requirements for the company.

First flag: Terry hired three people to take on the advertising sales job that I alone had been doing for 10 years. Hire One was the wife of a man Terry already employed to handle the technical web aspects of Healthline. Her only professional experience? Peddling air fresheners to offices. Hire Two was a friend of one of Terry's minions, whose prior work entailed cleaning out horse stalls. Hire Three was the most qualified, in that she'd worked part-time at a Montessori school. At least she was smart and familiar with the types of places (i.e. schools) *Local Living* was cultivating as potential advertisers.

Not one of Terry's hires had relevant sales experience. The plan was that I would train them, teach them about the sales process, help them with phone calls, and go with them to meet current and potential clients. I spent the next several months working with them individually and as a team while I was still doing sales for *Local Living*. Four months later, by October, not one of them had made a single sale.

This brings me to the second major red flag. In the four months since Terry had taken over ownership of the company, there had not been a single conversation between us. Nothing about her goals, her sales projections, her plans for what she wanted to do or how she wanted things to go. Although I see now how odd that was, at the time, for me, life at *Local Living* was business as usual. Can you imagine taking over a company and not having a single conversation with the prior owner, who still works for the company—the one who previously brought in all the revenue—about goals or strategies? Yeah. Neither can I.

I was running the business as it had always been run, including managing the editorial decisions, calling on advertisers, working on the layout with the designer. Nothing in terms of daily life had changed, except for the added burden of having to hand-hold three incompetent-for-the-job, non-sales people.

From Day One, Terry was lackadaisical on the topic of revenue. She never expressed concerns, set goals, or made targets for me or the other salespeople. Her lack of attention to the sales revenue was a huge concern for me, so I went about running the business as I always had: ever aware of what monthly numbers needed to be.

Terry had one minion, Mongo, already working for Healthline. This employee's lack of professionalism was apparent when she showed up to a luncheon wearing a grease-stained t-shirt draped beneath a raggedy flannel shirt. Mongo swiftly inserted herself into editorial and sales matters, stirring up shit that wasn't really there. Think Gladys Kravitz.

By October, things were officially weird. No organizational, sales, or strategic direction from Terry. I was running interference with Mongo about issues she knew nothing about (such as sales training techniques or closing $20,000 deals). The three "sales" people hadn't closed a single deal in months. Like a dark, unsettling fog you can't see but definitely feel, the sentiment in my gut was something wicked this way comes.

Since I'd initially agreed to financial terms thinking nothing could possibly go wrong, at that point I'd been paid a third of the total sale. Weekly meetings were taking place between myself and the sales people to get updates and offer support. After months of training, crafting emails on their behalf to prospects, creating phone call scripts, going with them to meetings, they still had not made a single sale between them. During extremely rare phone calls with Terry, I expressed serious concerns about their lack of progress.

Terry never indicated one way or another what she was going to do. She was loyal to one salesperson, the wife of her IT guy; the other was a friend of Mongo's, and it's fair to say Mongo was in Terry's ear.

The morning of December 17, 2014, a week before Christmas, I showed up at Terry's for a meeting she'd requested. IT guy was sitting at his desk. Helga was hiding behind a desk in the corner. After I arrived, I sat down on the couch and endured an awkward moment of silence. Terry then stood up and extended an envelope, saying the words, "We're done."

I wasn't quite sure what I was seeing or hearing. Then reality exploded like a bomb. I was being fired.

My blood sank into a warm pool of disbelief.

What?

I'm not even sure what I said in response, the shock was too much.

I'd only been fired once, when I was 24, for being late one too many times, and I'd deserved it. But this? Fired from the company I'd toiled over for a decade? For what? Not a single one of those two painful little words that took less than three seconds to vomit made sense. *We're. Done.*

A 10-year intimate relationship with the third love of my life, aside from my husband and children, had been instantly, unjustifiably, unexplainably severed.

It was hard to choose: grasp for the knife in my back or the one in my heart? I believe I pleaded with Terry, asked her why, blubbered that if there'd been problems, she could have come to me. I peered over at IT guy, who pretended to have his face buried in his computer. Then I glanced at Helga, who had known this was coming—I could tell by her cowardly hunch. She would have prepared the last kiss-of-death check that had traveled in the air from Terry's extended hand toward mine.

Then the oddest thing in an already extremely odd occurrence happened. Terry asked if she could give me a hug. I was too numb and shocked to move so she leaned in, bestowed a stiff embrace, then commanded me to leave.

And from a surreal *Goodbye Yellow Brick Road* moment, which simultaneously slipped by and stomped time, the only Me I'd ever known was detonated by two words: We're. Done. I was callously thrust over a cliff by a traveling envelope, as the winter solstice approached and I fell down, down, down, into an abyss of a dark and lonely Flight.

Flannels, a Crown & a Ring

Twenty minutes later I was home. By then, shock was making way for other emotions: sadness, disbelief, confusion, anger, more shock. Mark was home; it was his day off. I relayed what had happened. Protector that he is, he asked a lot of questions. *What happened? Why did you get fired? Did you know it was coming?* As he realized that I didn't have a single answer, the defender took over. *That bitch. How could she? Did Helga know? I can't believe it.*

It wasn't yet 2 p.m., but I got into my penguin flannel pajamas. I poured myself a stiff glass of Crown Royal. It's hard to explain how being in shock and numb and observing an exploding future can all co-mingle but that's what was happening.

There was much that transpired over the next few days and months, but I'll share a couple of highlights. The next week was Christmas, and boy oh boy did the sudden turn of events craft a damper. I didn't shower or even leave the pajamas for four days. Every day for the past several decades I'd woken up with a purpose. For 10 of those years I'd had a prominent title. I had an expectation to get dressed. There were meetings to go to, phone calls to return, emails to answer, deadlines to meet. Brushing teeth was part of a program. I had an understood place within the world about *who* I was and *how* I was. Identity was clear. Reasons for being, doing, breathing. None of those existed anymore. POOF! They died.

The hardest part was that I had no clue or foreshadowing as to *why?* In that five-month period, there hadn't been a single conversation in which Terry expressed concerns, asked questions, told me to do something differently, laid out a strategy, warned me of anything. That's what made everything such a stake to the heart. The action had no justification.

Christmas came and I was feeling pretty low. Since my kids are with their dad for Christmas Eve, Mark suggested we go out for dinner. I was in no mood but at least I showered. Instead of getting dressed in normal clothes, I compromised—from flannel pajamas to a sweatpants ensemble.

After a quiet night by the fireplace and some tequila sipping when we got back from Chinese food, my kids came home around 8:30 p.m. We have a tradition of opening one gift on Christmas Eve. Mark stepped out of the room and came back holding something behind his back. With a kid on each side, Mark got down on a knee and handed me a box with a ring in it. After nearly six years of being together, he'd asked me to marry him.

Within the span of a week, I'd had one of the strangest, saddest moments of my life followed by one of the most surprising, happiest moments of my life.

As year's end approached, questions loomed about the huge second payment Terry owed me by December 31. The clock was ticking. The marriage proposal glow was cut short as phone calls and meetings with lawyers began.

I'd written a five-page letter to Terry as a last-ditch effort to reason, clarify, something—to stave off further action I assumed neither of us wanted. I don't remember if I sent it or not.

I was referred to a business attorney from a divorce lawyer friend of mine. December 26 we were on the phone as I explained what had transpired only a week before. It felt like an eternity ago. I provided as many details as I could.

My attorney drafted demand letters to Terry's attorneys. There was no response, no contractually obligated payment was made, December 31 came and went, and the stage was set.

Three distinct, overwhelming, identity-influencing paths were simultaneously set into motion: 1) the complicated, ugly legal path that took years to resolve; 2) the beginning of my marriage to Mark; 3) the identity crash and launch into my Dark Flight of the Self.

To tidy up the background of how, when, and why my identity crash began, I'll simplify the legal path and only include aspects relevant to the other two paths, which are the focus of my story.

It became grossly apparent that Terry and her bags o' money team of expensive lawyers were gladly willing to help her dig in for a fight. Letters from attorneys went back and forth. Terry initially had a baseless claim for not paying; the burden to fulfill the contract was on her. But thanks to a single line that I had not seen within the initial contract (a line that would have surely been discovered if I'd had a lawyer at the outset), she'd bought a loophole to fill legal cracks.

In Lawyerland, time equals money. Terry figured she'd outlast and out-money me, because she could. I was already in the hole to my current attorney for $20,000. He believed my case would likely go to trial or at least close, and estimated the cost (gasp!) of such an outcome.

My wedding was coming up in March, and the idea of starting a marriage with a major legal situation didn't feel emotionally or financially fair to Mark. I couldn't bear the thought of bringing him onto a life honeymoon cruise on the Titanic.

Besides my identity crashing, I was living in constant fear. Fear of losing everything—my house, my dignity, my business that I'd worked so hard to build and had hoped to reap rewards from. I had no idea when any of it would end. Each week they'd buy time and trot out new ridiculous, hurtful, and untrue statements about what had transpired. The accusations about me and my character, and the assertions on which Terry was basing the claim were all part of an alternate universe. It was a crash course in how far someone will go with "alternative facts" to bury the truth.

The lies were constructed to create a legal maze that would put me in financial ruin to disprove. What's more, the ethics on which I'd built my business were under fire. They were concocting little nothings to cast doubt on my integrity and undermine my identity. This is why the legal path played such havoc with my Dark Flight. Everything I was and did was being wrongfully attacked. Welcome to the world of justice.

Taking advantage of spineless Helga, whom she now employed, Terry had coerced Helga into lying about some accounting things Terry had initially been provided prior to the sale. Even though facts could be proven in my favor because I had copies of everything, the tactic was to use Helga to insert a measure of doubt. Helga only cared about saving her own big Brutus hide.

My attorney knew that given Terry's strategy of making outlandish claims to stretch things out, I had no means to keep pace. He suggested I find another attorney who might be willing to lower his or her rate to take on my case. I was given a few referrals.

One guy was a Slick Willy douchebag who wore a thick gold chain around his neck, had a fake spray tan, and smelled like Brut 33. He looked me in the eye and said he might consider the case if, and only if, I could pay him $15,000 a month. I left his office in tears. Mark had gone with me and was so angry at Slick's smug attitude and how he had talked down to me that he said he wanted to kick Slick's ass.

After receiving preliminaries about the case, a second attorney, Hoffman, agreed to an appointment. Mark and I went to his office the next day. By this juncture, only a month after being married, the prospect of anything related to legal matters seemed emotionally and financially out of reach. I was losing time and hope. I was exhausted from worry, depression, fear, and the constant barrage of falsehoods being contrived by Terry's legal team.

Hoffman asked me to tell him what had happened. I spent the next hour crying, reliving, and going over details as best as I could. He told me he'd take the case on a contingency basis. He said he believed me and believed I'd been legally bullied and wronged.

Leaving Hoffman's office that morning was the first time in months I felt like I could breathe. I was grateful he believed me. Having someone stick his neck out to defend my honor was a godsend. I had legal protection from someone willing to stand by me and see it through without financial ruin, but even more important, Hoffman restored my faith in humanity.

* * * * *

Still on the legal path, the strife that hung over me made moving forward nearly impossible. Having my character attacked. Financial uncertainty. New claims to address, which required hours of digging up refuting evidence. Would my Dark Flight have been any shorter or different if I hadn't felt paralyzed by the legal cloud looming over me?

Over the next year and a half (as emails between Helga and Terry were submitted as evidence), I learned the betrayals that had transpired, the petty jealousies of Mongo and her tactics to turn others against me.

Perhaps the most difficult injustice was facing both Terry and Helga for depositions, 18 months later.

Anger seethed in me, sitting across a table from each of them. It was one of the hardest aspects of the entire debacle. I'd spent months in repression, and it was surreal to defend my character and try to make sense of what I knew were lies concocted for harm. I never doubted my truth, but I learned that when it comes to the law, "truth" can show many faces and that scared me. In my mind, there was only one truth. My business was sold on good faith, in good standing. In law, however, the truth wasn't what mattered.

Could I command my skin to magically thicken?

I told my mind to stop spinning, to not think about how much time and energy had been robbed, to not speculate on causes—psychic, karmic, or logical—for what had happened.

I was mad at myself for allowing the attack on my integrity and how it had undermined my belief in myself, my confidence.

How is it that other people handle life's challenges with grace and fortitude and I allowed the darkness in? I allowed it to weaken and overtake my sense of singularity.

Before arriving at the depositions, I listened to *Death on Two Legs* by Queen. Twice. The words were fitting and cathartic. Hoffman consoled me before going into the room by sharing that no matter the outcome, what we were doing would never feel like justice.

* * * * *

The trial was scheduled for July. Depositions had taken place in May and revealed that even though I'd been robbed, there were problematic legal soft spots. In June, a conversation about mediation began. In theory, mediation brings two opposing parties closer toward agreement to avoid a trial that would be emotionally taxing, expensive, and perhaps uncertain in its outcome.

I was willing to go to trial, though. I felt strongly about being in the right, but Hoffman warned that juries don't always understand business matters and it would only take one or two people in a selected pool to have doubt and I could go home empty-handed.

Mediation was conducted by a crotchety retired judge. The parties were placed in two separate yet adjoining rooms. Back and forth, back and forth, back and forth; it was an auction house. Terry owed me a lot and started with an offer of nothing. Ten hours was required to fill in blanks between what I was owed and what would be paid. I discovered that the mediator's job wasn't to find agreeable terms, it was to scare the shit out of me so I'd give in.

Hoffman was steadfast and by the end of a very long, adrenaline-filled yet exhausting day, the damn thing was settled. I wasn't happy, not by a long stretch, but that portion of the chapter, the path of the legalese, was mostly over. Terry milked hassle and cruelty till the last drop. What was supposed to be paid within two weeks took three months to receive. As expected, *Local Living* died a few months after this war was over.

* * * * *

Some Notes

Legal muck took years. I couldn't move on because I was in a strange holding pattern. I was anxious from the toxic cloud surrounding me. Most of Me went with the identity crash—my confidence, optimism, naiveté. These were attributes that served me in the professional realm.

I floundered for months in a space of separateness—from my body, my mind, my will. To offer a glimpse of my internal struggles between judgment, expectation, and emotional paralysis, the following are a few of my notes from that time.

NOTE 1:

Not my best day. I got up around 8:30 a.m. I've been sick with a nasty cold since Wednesday, the day Mark left to visit a friend in Texas. I haven't been out of the house for four days. This is the time of the month bills have to be paid. I've avoided balancing the checkbook because I'm afraid of what I'll find.

I printed out the bank register, sat on the floor and reviewed expenses. Our joint account has -$97.36, my personal account has -$162.17. I have no money coming in for the next several weeks. Bills overdue: water, gas, cable, electricity, and attorney. I feel ashamed, backed into a corner, and my stomach is swelling with panic. What now? How could I have let it come to this? I've been emotionally drowning for months.

I used to see myself as a high-powered executive. It's not that I see myself as ineffective or unmotivated. The problem is I just don't see myself at all. Being invisible has paralyzed me. I'd go if I knew where to go. It seems most people know most things as they relate to themselves. They know they're unhappy. They know they're tired. They have awareness about whatever it is they're feeling or going through. Even if it's an unpleasant knowing. My mind, my body, my emotions, my thoughts, everything is disconnected and floating.

NOTE 2:

It's possible to become addicted to wallow. I've stretched to clever internal lengths to explain the Peter Brady pity parade I've become. I am all dressed up, wearing a bad harvest-gold tie and awful pea-green suit, waiting for a surprise party that's not to be.

There's validity to sadness when big change happens. But after a certain point, there's nothing left to do but change channels. I'm actually sick of myself. I've officially run out of ways to lament. I've exhausted all catchphrases for "poor me." My name is Janna and I'm a wallow addict.

"Wallow" is intentionally used as a noun, not as a verb, as in wallow-*ing*. Wallow has become a thing, an entity unto itself, that while unattractive and most certainly unproductive, provides a measure of camaraderie. Like two old drunks sitting on stools in a musty, smoky dive bar, alone but together.

What supports my suspicion that I'm a wallow addict is that as stressed, depressed, and lost as I feel, I take no substantive action to change anything. I watch myself tumble. Today I feel so damn small. I heard that our Oregon Zoo's beloved Packy, an elephant, died. Why should this matter? Yet I'm in tears, inconsolable. Everything changes. Everything dies.

NOTE 3:

I'm on my second beverage. Pendleton bourbon neat. I can't tell you the last night without a cocktail. At least one if not two. It's 7:36 p.m. I'm ready for bed. There are mothers out there, better mothers than me, making the most of this time. Cleaning out a closet. Attending a PTA meeting. Making a nutritious meal. Baking cupcakes for their children's class.

Do I truly hate myself? What did I ever do?

NOTE 4:

Last night I had a dream. I was beneath a train looking up at the axle as the long rusty bar hovering above started to move. In fear, I watched the heavy wheels squealing forward. I was trying to figure out how to escape from beneath an about-to-be-moving train to avoid getting crushed. Time and escape were of the essence. Yet I didn't move.

Hearing people's dreams is as interesting as a wallet accordion filled with photos of someone's kid. Yet it revealed my internal conflict. I know many people are afraid—but afraid of what? That was the question. It's why I think the depth of identity loss and grief I'm talking about is different than most social conversations. I feel exposed—open to foreign elements in a scary, sitting-duck way. I'm internally stripped. I don't love the word "vulnerable," but I will concede to vulnerability, as in defenseless, accessible, and weak.

I'm swimming in an ocean without a shoreline in view. I'm donning a white jumpsuit while trudging through a blizzard. I'm aimlessly flying toward exhaustion.

* * * * *

I want to run away.

I wish there was a refuge where lost women in Dark Flight who needed a small place to land, women who've flapped 'til emotional wings shed, could gather.

And when you feel like I feel, you hitch a ride on a plane, drive or crawl and within a few hours descend to the refuge where you harvest burdens of your mind and unravel them and leave them at a forgiveness altar for a week, two weeks, months, maybe even a day. I'm not thinking the escape is for gourmet meals, I'm begging for a sweet freedom to fall apart without concern of watchful eyes.

Imagine if there was such a place where you could escape and have space to breathe without judgment or expectation to see

where your mind takes you,

your body takes you,

what your heart shows you,

and the beautiful mess you'd create if you lucidly

fell apart.

Would I meekly shatter, piece by piece, one layer at a time, one heartbreak, one expectation, one responsibility, or will the finale be far more spectacular as I implode?

Soaring Back to School

Once legal logistics were over, I had a puff of air to think about what was next. My friend Karen had had a great experience back in school, redefining her life at Marylhurst University. Each time we talked she'd happily reveal new ideas she'd opened to. Karen had made more progress in the few years she'd been a student at Marylhurst than in the 13 years I'd known her. Her unfolding inspired me.

In Portland, Marylhurst was known for being an adult-learner sanctuary, for those with busy lives who were seeking to complete unfinished degrees. A beautiful older campus made brick by brick, nestled in a grove of old oak, willow, and pine trees, and founded by nuns more than 125 years earlier, Marylhurst was a peaceful place.

* * * * *

A bit about my history with education. I took the proficiency exam at 16 and dropped out of high school. There were friends to party with, low-wage jobs to get hired and fired from, a crazy boyfriend five years older than I to hang out with, and the real kicker—I thought I was smarter than all that. An immature, know-it-all girl with a nowhere plan.

Once that non-plan turned problematic, Santa Monica City College became my on-again, off-again default. I'd take a class, drop a class. Take a class, not show up. Take a class, sorta be interested. When I retrieved transcripts to apply at Marylhurst in the summer of 2016, the record showed I did the SMCC dance over 12 years. From 1984–1996. I was mortified and found it humorous to ask, "Who the fuck goes to community college for 12 years?"

By my early 30s, I had moved to Portland and the thought of school hung around, so I had enrolled at Portland State University. I applied for and got a full scholarship to PSU based on my ethnic diversity. I took my Jew-ritto status of being a good Mexican Jew and made matzoh ball chorizo with my education. I was grateful. At 31, I got serious about school. I went full-time as an English major and worked part-time as a communications coordinator for a nonprofit called Children First for Oregon. For the first time in my academic life, I was doing well in school, getting straight A's. I was not going to squander the opportunity I'd been provided.

October 1999, I decided to start my own PR consulting business and finish my last school year while working for myself. I'd made some contacts in the nonprofit world, there was a need for PR services, and I loved working with organizations that helped children and families. Only a few months later, on January 1, 2000, my pregnancy test had a +. The news changed everything.

I stayed in school winter and spring terms, while pregnant, but by summer (I was due in August), I'd put school on hold. I had my beautiful daughter, Violet, and, well, life got busy. I worked from home as my baby did what babies do: cry, get fed and changed, be loved. Being a mother took getting used to, but I fell hard and instantly into motherly love.

Weeks of school absence melted into months, then years. I had Ethan four years later. My consulting business was making enough to support my family. Then I bought *Local Living*. School became a memory. I was supporting two kids, running a business, and thought, "Who needs school?" There seemed to be no point in going into debt to get a piece of paper when I was doing fine.

Fast forward another lost decade. I sold *Local Living*, the sale was a bust, I was in turmoil, and my life, identity, and direction were aimless. I didn't have a next. At nearly 50, there were no answers, only questions. I thought I'd inquire at Marylhurst to see how much school I had left. I guessed roughly a year to finish. After transcripts were evaluated, I was right.

With knowledge that I only had a year to go, I couldn't *not* finish. I also realized that the routine I'd been in for a decade didn't require anything new of me, per se. Midlife is probably an ideal time to learn how to learn again.

My transcripts, however, spanning over 25 years, were like a drunken Tweety Bird tattoo of data, and prompted humiliation.

With mixed feelings, I applied to Marylhurst in the summer of 2016. The admissions staff was amazing, especially a woman named Victoria. She held my emotional hand as I was overwhelmed by the prospect of being back in school. Perhaps I was reminded of how aimless I'd felt, or had regret that I didn't finish school earlier, or saw how directionless I'd been; I had a lump in my throat every time I had to do a logistical task for the enrollment process. I'd call Victoria crying and she'd talk me off the ledge.

On June 7, 2016, I got the email that I'd been admitted to Marylhurst and felt a surge of warm excitement. To soften the financial commitment, Marylhurst was generous with financial help. Two combined scholarships (one from the Knight Foundation and the other a Binford writing scholarship) took care of half of my tuition. Those supports made school feasible; I took out loans for the rest.

Going back to school was a way to swim. I had no idea where I was swimming from or to, there were no shorelines in sight, but revisiting education was a way to move my arms and legs to save myself from drowning. The motion of being in motion counted for something, something important I could not yet see.

Having someplace to go a few nights a week prevented me from going to bed at 7 p.m.—a step in the right direction. I was exposed to thoughts and ideas and conversations outside my own circle of warbling; sometimes you just gotta cut yourself off from the pity. I think this is what going to school prompted: a self-imposed moratorium from myself.

I signed up for three classes in the fall of 2016: two on-campus night classes and one online course. Initially balancing work and going to school was difficult. I'd been independent for so long that a requirement of being somewhere at a specific time several nights a week fostered resentment. I didn't like the obligation to homework. My inner child wanted to tell my professors, "You're not the boss of me!"

While I complained as I sat in traffic two nights a week, I was also more inspired than I'd been in a long time. Being in the classroom, engaged in deep dialog with other thoughtful people and presented with new ideas, intellectually ignited me. I felt brought back to life mentally, and in some ways, creatively.

That year was a constant push and pull between resentment and excitement about being back in school. I was angry for not finishing earlier in life, yet inspired by other adult learners who'd braved going back to school. These women and a few men had diverse stories about where they'd been, who they were, what they hoped to accomplish. The focus, sacrifice, and self-love I saw in classmates were beautiful to witness. If you've ever gone back to school later in life and been among older adult learners, you know what I'm talking about. If you've ever thought about going back to school, I highly encourage it for this reason alone. To observe the grit, commitment, and sacrifice of fellow students is incredible. Each person had their own complicated story of who they'd been and the wild dream of who they hoped to become. It was only the dream they saw.

* * * * *

One night after a writing class, I had a breakthrough. The class discussion had been related to the author Ta-Nehisi Coates, themes of identity, and Coates's book, *Between the World and Me*. My professor Jay Ponteri asked us to consider how we see ourselves in the world and the various selves that we have. I had a hard time seeing myself at all, which made the conversation fuzzy. But something Jay said stuck: "We're never really any one self but rather expressions of many selves that show up from time to time."

On the drive home I reflected on how that related to me. It was true that at one time I had been highly productive. That was a "self" I knew. The productive self that showed up in the world was from necessity—I did what I had to do to run my business. That form of my self didn't originate from a foundation of my being, but rather, as a byproduct of my *doing*. That self was created as a means of survival.

Yet, I was conflicted. Without stress, who was I? Was it possible to have a level of purpose without a high level of stress caused by a need to be productive? What I missed most about the professional life, my identity at that time, was engagement. As a publisher, I was involved with the world. Once the title ended, the work ended, the purpose ended, I became isolated. But maybe that highly productive self was no longer me. I'd been so hard on myself, I felt like a failure, inadequate, because I hadn't been "productive."

The realization was that being productive might have been my Self at one time, out of necessity. So what if I was unproductive? That didn't say anything about who I am, although I'd taken it so personally.

That breakthrough slightly loosened a self-imposed noose. Thanks to the school structure and educational inquiry, such morsels fed my hungry spirit during my year at Marylhurst. For all the emotional gifts education brought me as an adult learner, and the ways in which going back to school refilled my identity coffers, I would encourage you to go back to school if you've ever thought about it. This act of courage and self-love will never be regretted.

* * * * *

June 24, 2017, I became part of something I never thought I would: the world of college graduates. I'd realized a dream I didn't even know I had. On the morning of commencement ceremonies, I rose before everyone in the house to enjoy a solitary cup of coffee. I watched the hummingbirds outside. The sun came up beyond the trees and lit up the yard a hopeful gold. My stomach flipped as I thought about the extraordinary thing I was about to do: put on a cap and gown, tassel and medallion. I would soon experience a moment that was 30 years in the making.

It was gratifying to have my children see me accomplish this goal. They could recognize their mother as a college graduate. Mark had been supportive and I knew he was proud that I'd done it. I felt giddy. I had done something great. Defenses over feeling like a failure subsided. I finished college with a total GPA of 3.90.

That quiet morning, as I placed the graduation cap on my head, I looked in the mirror. Who I saw wasn't someone new, but she was unfamiliar. The reflection showed me someone I didn't know—a college graduate.

How Can There Be
a "We" When There's
Nothing of "Me"?

I'm 20 years late on the *Gilmore Girls* bandwagon. Mark and I were visiting my friend Larry in Las Vegas and the first day we arrived I got food poisoning. By 2 p.m. I was relegated to the guest room air mattress and running to the bathroom every five minutes.

There was no TV in the guest room, but thanks to a laptop and Netflix, I had options. I'm picky when it comes to streaming TV. I don't watch shows that rely on sex, violence, or betrayal, which leaves out nearly everything.

I scrolled through the selections and there was *Gilmore Girls*. I'd read that the writer of *The Marvelous Mrs. Maisel* (which I loved!), Amy Sherman-Paladino, was also the writer for *Gilmore Girls*. From the first episode, I was hooked. The writing was sharp and as a mom who was navigating life with my own smart, accomplished, beautiful teen-aged daughter—the same premise as the show—I could relate.

In the series, the on-again, off-again love relationship between Lorelei (the main character, played by Lauren Graham) and Luke (another main character, played by Scott Patterson) was similar to how I sometimes experienced my marriage.

Lorelei and Luke have different temperaments, different ways of seeing the world, yet are compatible. Lorelei is self-sufficient, makes her own decisions, occasionally puts up barriers for emotional protection, but needs demonstrative reassurance even though she won't admit it. Lorelei is emotionally complicated. She questions things and wants understanding.

Luke is a basic what-you-see-is-what-you-get type of personality. Doesn't need frills or extras. He's hardworking. He's loyal, dependable, and will always do the right thing. He keeps most of his interior world, thoughts, and expressions to himself. When push comes to shove, Luke may reveal a slice or two about what he's feeling, but he assumes that everyone should just know where he stands. Because of how they are,

Luke and Lorelei have many star-crossed moments of missed signals. Yeah. Luke and Lorelei? Mark and me.

Mark and I met online in November of 2010. I'd gotten divorced the summer of that year. My daughter was 10 and my son was six. I was 43 and had not been in the dating scene for over 13 years. I had no idea what type of commodity I'd be in the open market. Over the decade I was married, online dating had become a thing. I thought I'd try it. With the holidays approaching, days were cold and dark. I was lonely.

Mark first "winked" and sent a message introducing himself on the evening of Monday, November 22. From his picture (which was small), it was hard to tell what he looked like but he seemed to have a nice smile. I replied with a hello.

Mark's profile revealed he was also 43, a widower and father of a 13-year-old daughter. We appeared to have similar interests. He started an online conversation with me. Mark seemed warm, casual, easy to chat with. When the conversation veered toward our careers, I shared I was the publisher of a magazine. He asked which one and I replied, "*Local Living.*"

Every September the *Local Living* issue was dedicated to lengthy features about women's cancers—breast, ovarian, thyroid, cervical—which included treatments, doctors making a difference and stories about women navigating their diseases. Offering education about women's cancers was an editorial topic I was passionate about.

The September 2007 issue of *Local Living* had focused on the personal stories of five women in various stages of a cancer journey. As it turned out, one of the five women in that feature story was Holley, Mark's wife. She had died six months after the story was published. The feature had pictures of him, her, and their daughter, Shelly. When I told him I owned *Local Living*, he was as surprised by the coincidence, as I was. He shared how much it meant to Holley to have her story published. That was nice to know.

Mark revealed he'd been at Intel for 15 years as a hazardous gas pad technician (took me years to figure out what that actually meant). He worked the 7 p.m. to 7 a.m. shift because it was quiet at night and he had time to dink around the internet. I mentioned that if he wanted to get to know me better, he could peruse my Facebook page and I shared the link. I had a bunch of photos I'd taken, poems I'd written to wade through the post-divorce aftermath, and observations related to current events.

I typed to Mark that if he was still interested in connecting with me after seeing my Facebook page, he could call me. I gave him my phone number.

The next day at 2 p.m., my phone rang. It was a call that changed my life.

His voice was deep, with a loose ease. Mark told me that he had spent most of the night reading everything about me on my Facebook page, including the archive of recent poems. He said he was impressed with my writing and reiterated the strangeness of the *Local Living* article coincidence.

We talked for an hour about things we liked to do, our kids, our jobs. The connection got real when we discovered we both liked '80s hair metal music. As phone call first dates go, ours was a success. I felt giddy in a way I hadn't in over 15 years. Mark had to get ready for work that night and asked if he could call me later. I said okay.

The next few days were a flurry of teenage texting, online chats, and phone calls. The mutual attraction was clear and it was agreed we'd meet in person. Thursday was Thanksgiving and the following day Mark was flying with buddies to Oakland to check out a Raiders football game. He was scheduled to be gone until Monday night, then had work Tuesday and Wednesday nights. We arranged to have lunch on Thursday, December 2.

The night before Thanksgiving, Mark called and said he didn't want to wait that long to meet me. My kids were scheduled to be with their dad for the holiday and it was the first year I would be alone. I'd not been looking forward to being without my children, so I'd made plans to meet friends for a few drinks and listen to music at the Dublin Pub. Mark was having dinner with family.

We arranged for a 6 p.m. rendezvous—a slot squeezed in after his meal with his family and before my drinks with the girls.

Thanksgiving Day, I felt blue. I missed Ethan and Violet. I got in the shower to get ready for my first real date in years. At that point in my life, I'd been going to the gym for three years, six days a week at 5 a.m. I was strong and fit, and tight-fitting jeans were my power suit. I chose my favorite pair, some black pointy-toed boots, and a cute black vest, with a black lace camisole underneath. I can say with some assurance that it didn't matter what I was wearing, it didn't take much to look good.

When I drift back to that Thanksgiving night, remembering the reflection of who I saw in the mirror years ago, I feel sad. That image of me, the me I was then, seems light years ago. Where the fuck did that hot-looking, confident, ambitious, magazine-owning publisher, rockin'-jeans-wearing, not-a-single-gray-hair-in-sight, wrinkle-free woman go?

About 5:45 p.m., I hopped into a new car I'd splurged on. Three weeks earlier I'd gotten rid of the Toyota Sienna minivan (which was sooooo cliché, and a car I never wanted in the first place). That symbol of my past life was forsaken for a used, forest-green BMW 328i. I blasted a Scorpions CD. I replayed conversations from the past few days. I was 16 again. At 5:55, I pulled into the nearly empty parking lot of the Dublin Pub and parked next to the only other vehicle there, a silver

Toyota Tacoma truck. Mark got out on his side and walked around to me as I stood up. He tucked his arm gently behind my waist and surprised me with a soft kiss hello.

As I pulled away, I took in his face to absorb the entity I'd been flirting with by text. *Hmmmm . . . he's cuter than his pictures.* That moment of mutual size-up between us was awkward and sweet. It's been eons since I've recalled it.

Dublin Pub was not yet open but it was Thanksgiving, so alternatives were few. Across the street was another pub, Raleigh Hills McMenamins. It was open. My friends were scheduled to show at the Dublin around 8 p.m.

Mark and I sat in a large wooden booth. He ordered some sort of thick beer; I got a Jack 'n' Diet Coke. When the waiter asked if we were ordering food, Mark glanced at me and said he was full from dinner. I recalled I was alone, and without my kids, for that first Thanksgiving, peered at the menu, and settled on tater tots and a small salad.

For the next few hours, we got lost in the newness of each other. Meandering between details about Holley's cancer, my divorce, his job at Intel, mine at *Local Living*, first concerts, my saga of owning a minivan, why I chose a BMW, his life in Forest Grove, mine in L.A., who our friends were, his longtime love of the Raiders, favorite bands, and probably a hundred other forgettable details that seemed like the most important things in the world because they belonged to us.

From that first hello kiss and throughout our conversation, I felt at home. By 8 p.m., I was toasty from two Jack 'n' Cokes and raging chemical currents. We rambled across the street where my friends Cassie, Alisha, and Charlie were waiting. I'd informed the ladies of my date prior to the Dublin, and they could see by how Mark and I clung to each other that the date was going well.

I introduced Mark to everyone as we joined the girls at the table. When I reflect back on that night, I remember how good I looked in those jeans, how much fun we had, and how comfortable I felt from the first moment of Mark's presence.

I stopped drinking around 9 p.m. because I had to drive. By 11 p.m., our crowd had thinned and *the* unspoken moment arrived. How would the rest of the night unfold? My kids were with their dad, it was Thanksgiving, I was lonely, I was single, and it had been hard to keep our paws off each other. We strolled to our cars, where the night had begun. It seemed impossible that it had only been five hours before with all I felt, how much we'd connected.

Mark came in for the goodnight kiss and I whispered, "I don't live far from here . . ." He looked slightly surprised but pleased and said, "Okay, I'll follow you."

I watched his Toyota's headlights in my rearview mirror. That was probably the most anticipatory, butterfly-ridden, 8-minute drive I've ever had. Every female hormone I'd produced in my 43 years was on fire. Desire swam throughout the interior of that BMW every second I got closer to home.

Our first night together was fantastic. Physically, the shape of Mark, his stature, his feel, his smell, his touch were all different than my ex-husband's. I'd been with Billy for nearly 13 years, but our last year together we'd had sex twice. It had been a while since I'd been physical and it was strange being with another man.

Aside from all the frolicking that transpired, there were other aspects of our first night that were magical. At about 2 a.m., we got out of bed, gulped down a gallon of water, raided the refrigerator for snacks and chowed down while listening to '80s hair metal—including Tesla, Def Leppard and Great White—from my iPad.

I was at ease in a way I'd never been before. After another go-around welcomed the rising sun, we fell into an entangled slumber for two hours. Then Mark had to get up to prepare for his football weekend in Oakland.

As he gathered his clothes, I robed and made coffee. There were no feelings of strangeness or regret. Everything was right. We lingered in the goodbye; he promised to call. Once I shut the door, a rush flooded in: the exhausted giddiness of staying up all night, the absence of my kids in the house, the pain of a new crush, the physical sensations of having too much sex after prolonged celibacy, the curiosity of how I'd felt so comfortable so soon, and the joy of feeling seen by a man.

Here, years later, I mourn the loss of that first night. The loss of the beautiful, fit, confident, sexy me that was then. And the loss of us, our birth as a couple, and the preciously fresh, magical awakening of our relationship.

* * * * *

When I met Mark, despite our joyful early days, he was mired in grief. Holley had been sick with cancer for a few years and he'd endured the uncertainty of watching someone he loved in constant pain. I got a glimpse into cancer's heartbreak through stories about her physical and emotional ups and downs and the effects they'd had on him and their daughter. All the hospital visits. All the treatments. All the side effects. All the planning that went into getting affairs in order once Holley knew she was terminal. All the sadness of being by Holley's side as she gasped her last breath—that, of all the things, haunted Mark the most.

He was shut down, numb from loss, and had a suitcase of grief-anger that occasionally popped open. Coming from a pull-yourself-up-by-the-bootstraps, counseling-is-for-crazy-people world, Mark had never received grief support. Everyone, including Holley, had told Mark he'd be fine. But when he wasn't—because who can be "fine" after watching someone you love die a horrible, painful death—all that stuff got bottled up, with nowhere to go.

Meeting me, wanting a life with me, and having new feelings and ideas became an internal tug-of-war for Mark. In his eyes, I was an exciting woman: the publisher of a magazine who took him to fancy events, introduced him to prominent people (I'll never forget how excited he was to meet Ann Schatz, also known as Running Ann, a sports commentator Mark grew up following), and whisked him away from Forest Grove and into Publisherland. One can imagine how different that would be.

Mark wasn't a country bumpkin, but he had lived a steadily rural existence for most of his life. He picked strawberries in the field as a boy. He had friends who drank Hamm's in barns, chewed tobacco, and had dead animal trophy heads hanging from their walls. I joked with Mark that he did all the farm boy "n's": fishin', huntin', shootin', barbequein', swimmin' . . . This fundamental difference in our upbringings has shown up in both positive and negative ways.

None of what I share is meant to place judgments on Mark. However, these differences affect our marriage. I struggle with how to balance fundamental personality differences, my expectations of a partner, and how to learn acceptance. I'm aware that if it wasn't this set of problems with Mark, it would just be a different set with someone else. No relationship is free of differences.

I also acknowledge that sharing these issues is selfish and self-indulgent. My hope is not to expose attributes that prompt judgment, but to shed light and move ahead with our marriage in a renewed, kinder way. I want to find my way back.

Have the past few years been rocky because I've gone through my Dark Flight?

Are we growing apart?

Have Mark and I always been fundamentally different, and now it's biting us in the ass?

How do people who are different find commonalities within a marriage?

Where does a line get drawn over being *too* different?

What kinds of differences ruin a marriage?

What kinds of differences strengthen it?

Where are the bridges to connect divides?

I'd really love to find answers to these questions.

In the first few years we were together, Mark was in the middle of his own Dark Flight identity meltdown. As his life got swept up in mine, it meant he'd have to leave his other one behind. In his mind, the closer he got to me, the further he got from Holley. He wanted to hold onto her. Ensuring distance from me, he clung to her.

Although the towns were only 20 minutes apart, life in Beaverton was vastly different than it was in Forest Grove. Beaverton was a city, with traffic, people, malls. Forest Grove was rural, with farms, neighbors who make jam, ma 'n' pa stores. Then there was the whole friends thing. My group of friends was unlike his. He blended into my circles okay, although it took time. I didn't blend into his. None of his friends liked me. We had nothing in common.

Mark brought me to barn parties and I'd be completely uncomfortable, with not a single thing to talk about with any of the wives or girlfriends who sat around smoking cigarettes, drinking beer from a can. I couldn't grasp any common ground. They thought I was trying to city-fy Mark.

As Mark straddled his former, current, and future lives, he had a lot of circumstances that forced a shift within his own identity. I watched the internal struggle unfold for years. Sometimes he embraced the changes, sometimes he didn't.

When it got to be too much, Mark got scared, as familiar ground crumbled beneath his feet. He'd find a reason to leave, or more specifically, break up with me. His leaving was abrupt, unforeseen, and explosive. This was incredibly unsettling for my kids, and I'll always regret that I didn't do more to protect them emotionally. It's unfortunate when our kids become entangled with our grown-up imperfections and missteps.

Mark got creative in his justifications of his self-detonation. His reasons never made sense. He knew he was afraid, and his emotions were overwhelming, but he couldn't verbalize them. Instead, he took the bottled-up fear and blew the fucker up.

This happened three times over the course of a few years. Each breakup lasted about a month, although the third and final one lasted for three months. Mark's third departure was just a few weeks after my father Joe suddenly dropped dead on his kitchen floor (an entirely fitting end for him) after losing his heart to an attack.

* * * * *

It was May 16, a Thursday morning, 9:15 a.m., when my phone rang. It was Connie, my dad's wife. I thought maybe she was calling to tell me he was in the hospital—years of smoking and drinking meant he'd not been a picture of health—but my dad was an Energizer bunny. He always kept going. So when she said, "Your father died," I was sure I'd heard something else.

Everything—sounds, motion, sights—warped into bodily shock. What? Wait. Huh???? My father was . . . dead?

Primal cries emitted from somewhere within me.

Calls were made to my older brother, Len, and my mother. I remember a blur of packing Ethan and Violet into my car and driving to L.A.

Mark came along. I later learned he had planned to break up with me, but dammit if my father hadn't fucked up his plans. With both of his feet already out the door (unbeknownst to me), we made the 16-hour trek from Portland.

Here's a sad part to an already sad story. My father had told Connie that when his time came, he didn't want a funeral. So no funeral was planned. There was no gathering of friends. No gathering of family. No words spoken about who my dad had been in life. No collective tears of goodbye. Acknowledgment of his life's passing was completely nonexistent and fully nondescript. I was a newly inaugurated fatherless child with nowhere to go. Losing a parent is a tremendous blow, defining who we become after that singular moment.

My dad and mom got married when they were 18. They were young, and the relationship was rocky from the start. They lasted long enough to create two children, my brother Len, then me three years later. They got divorced at 23. The separation was tumultuous, which meant my brother and I became casualties of anger. The result was that the first time I recall seeing my father was when I was about six years old. When the day came to meet for the first time as a child, I remember searching my closet for the prettiest dress I could find. I wanted him to like me.

After slipping on my best tights and brushing my hair, I went to the living room window to stare and nervously wait. After what felt like forever, an old, rusted Chevy pickup truck pulled into the driveway. A man I didn't know was walking toward the door and my heart pounded. He was sort of tall, with darker skin. The bell rang and after the door opened, all my strength and excitement and resolve disappeared and I no longer wanted to see him. My six-year-old mind was scared, hurt, and angry that he had never before wanted me, shy before this stranger, and I didn't want to leave my mother. I cried the moment it was time to go with him for the day.

The truck cab that my brother and I were crammed into smelled of stale cigarettes and cologne. Propped up like a poof of yellow frosting in my pretty taffeta dress, I was scared shitless sitting next to him. He told us he was taking us to a museum and a gem show. That didn't seem fun. I just wanted to go to McDonald's, get a Happy Meal, and go home. When I mustered the nerve to glance in his direction, I saw his dark skin was rough, like leather. I didn't think I looked like him. The old Chevy was noisy, rattling along, and I felt trapped. I looked over at my brother to see what he was thinking. He stared out the window.

I recall throughout the day, as we looked at boring old rocks and boring old bones, I tried to force myself not to be so scared and to be more funny and charming so my dad would like me.

My father lived a mile and a half away. We only saw him twice a year. For the entirety of my childhood, I never understood why. He had another family, his wife Connie and her daughter Lisa. I filled my head with all kinds of childish fantasies about how he was a better father to her and she was a better daughter for him. When it came to my dad, I always doubted myself, always perceived rejection, always felt like the 6-year-old who wanted him to like me. My father was just as uncomfortable with us, but he did his best to show love and affection, and to be there in the ways he was able.

Things shifted when I was in my early 20s. I tried to be an adult, to extend beyond our superficial dialog and have more authentic conversations. It was slow at first, but over the years we made progress. We periodically spent more time together. I got to know more about the man he was and see more of the father he might have been. He told me on numerous occasions how sorry he was for not being there, and how extremely proud of me he was. Those words were oxygen. I wish we could have had more time together. I'm wiser now. Maybe I would understand what questions to ask to know him better. I miss his laugh and I miss the love we were working on.

When you lose a parent, time liquidates; through death, the entire complicated, curvy road of a relationship with that parent somehow straightens. Years later, certain knowable edges fuzzed, while those in my heart rounded. Joe Lopez seemed indestructible. He had survived much in his rugged life as an only child raised by sick and alcoholic parents. He was the first person his friends would call for a favor; made the best tamales I've ever had. He approached life's unpredictable imperfections with humor. He learned to map coordinates of life traveled like the reliable cartography of pages in his well-worn Thomas Guide, stored in a console of his equally reliable Astro van. He was an amazing chef, true artist, and lover of art.

Although my father and I positively patched our relationship, the unceremonious marking of his death mirrored the way I felt about us as father and daughter for most of my life—as a secondary afterthought. My father left no will—one more representation of being unacknowledged. He was cremated. Before leaving L.A., I'd asked Connie for some ashes, to have some tangible piece of him and acknowledge both his death and life—to hold my own personal funeral. She initially said no, which was devastating, but months later she mailed a small, round margarine container filled with my father's ashes. I eventually spread them on the floor of my wedding altar.

* * * * *

Empty-handed and empty-hearted, Mark, my kids, and I made the long drive back to Portland after a few awkward days hanging around Los

Angeles. With no funeral, no ceremony, no acknowledgment, no will, no ashes, it was like my dad's death was a passing cloud of invisible smoke.

Mark broke up with me two days after we got back from Los Angeles. Crazy, huh?

The act of deserting his girlfriend right after her father has died shows how destructive Mark's identity crash was. That was one messed-up summer. (*D*eath, *d*estruction, *d*ismantling.)

Until then, my connection with Mark was a feeling-truth as opposed to a thinking-truth. I *felt* we belonged together. I'd never trusted, let alone heard, what my heart said. After Mark left, I wondered, *How I could have been so wrong?* If what my heart said was untrue and that kind of knowing was wrong, what part of my inner voice or heart could I ever trust?

Mark's third exit was awful. Heartbroken, I was confused about what could ever be known as true. The following story was something I wrote during that time. It described the circumstances of losing my father and Mark.

7/29/2013 - Leave It In The Clouds

There are many ways to wade through grief. Sometimes when you're at your lowest, an opportunity to chuck it all to the wind is one answer. A casual Friday night bar conversation with my friend Jojo about skydiving funneled into that opportunity. Today I jumped out of an airplane. I'm afraid to fly, I can't board a plane without Xanax, I'm terrified of heights, and I can't go near a window when inside a high-rise building.

In the last two months, my father Joe died and Mark left me. There's no convenient path around grief. My father had no funeral, according to his wishes, and Mark gave no warning of his exit. With both there was no "process" to process. Accordingly, my heart is wandering. No process only leaves ritual.

Tomorrow is my father's birthday. I was seeking a ritual to honor the passage. Then the Friday night conversation about skydiving happened. Perhaps skydiving would be a transformative action that transmutes grief. The more I thought about the metaphor of jumping into the unknown with nothing but faith and blue sky, the more it made sense. Take the ginormous inhale and then let it all go. Leave grief in the clouds.

I looked into skydiving and made an appointment for today. I didn't want to linger in anticipation. I didn't watch YouTube videos. I told one friend what I was doing, "just in case." Keeping hush was hard, but I didn't want the judgments of others to interfere with my experience.

As part of the ritual, I spent the morning searching for photos of my dad and Mark. There was even one of them together. On the back of each photo, I wrote something that needed to be said. I cut the photos into tiny scraps, placed them in a baggie, and stuck them in my back pocket to go along for the ride.

I arrived at Skydive Oregon at 11 a.m. I thought about my kids. I thought about not having a finished will. I wondered who would discover the private "goodies" in my bedroom should I plummet to my death. I mentally double-checked that I'd put on clean underwear that morning. Go figure.

Prospective jumpers are taken to a room for a 15-minute rundown of everything that can go hell-in-a-handbasket wrong with the plane, the jump, the parachute, the equipment. I learned some basic safety standards. Prior to reaching elevation, the instructor would ask, "Are you ready to jump out of the plane?" There can only be one answer: "Yes." You can't joke and say "No," you can't say "Maybe," you can't say "I hope so." There's only one answer. Otherwise, you're going back down as a return passenger in the plane, no refunds, no questions asked.

After training, I went outside and nervously watched another group go up. I was with a few other first-timers and some solo jumpers. By luck, I got paired with an instructor named Joe. Jumpers are literally attached to instructors' bodies as they plummet 18,000 feet.

Once suited up in appropriate gear, I crossed the runway to board a little plane with no doors on one side. We started a steep 10-minute climb toward 18,000 feet. Joe intensely attached the harness and parachute gear between us. I lowered the goggles over my eyes. It was an eternal 10 minutes as I watched the ground get smaller and smaller through the open door, knowing I'd soon be in the air just outside the plane. The moment arrived. Joe said, "Are you ready to jump out of the plane?" I nodded my head and choked out, "Yes."

We scooted on our butts across the plane floor, Joe directly behind me, inching toward the ledge. I looked down and saw nothing but tiny dots of land below and lots of sky and sun and I knew this was it and he said, "Go!" There was no time to think—I was falling. Like a water twister suctioned down a drain, down, down. Falling fast. The feeling in my stomach from the adrenaline, the speed, the force, and the vertigo of actually falling from the sky was unlike any other.

I was horizontal, like a bird peering down over the Earth. Square patches of farmland, like a tray of ice, edged closer, parallel with the curved horizon and slate of turquoise nothingness. We fell for a minute without a parachute, which was simultaneously the longest and shortest minute of my life. Joe tapped my shoulder to let me know he was releasing the parachute and with a slight jar and then pull of force, I was sailing, gratefully, with a colorful yellow chute above. I went from flying flat to dangling upright.

For the next six minutes, I took in the vast expanse of life below. My heart pounded, senses exploded. My cheeks were hot from the wind tunnel as we cascaded down the sky slide back to where we started. Joe maneuvered the parachute to get us in the right position with the wind flow, to safely land. I got nauseated from sailing the current.

We tumbled forward as our feet met ground and my stomach remained behind. I glanced up to verify that what I had just done was real, searching the sky toward the sun for traces of a broken heart left to mingle with the clouds.

The craziness of the third break-up period also included a night at a swing-er's club. I was out of my mind with grief. I include this story because it was part of unhinged expression of my identity loss. I believe it's common for some women to explore their own identities through sexuality, which may include physical/spiritual/sexual connection with other women. For me the curiosity was short-lived—one and done—yet it counts as a nota-ble piece of the puzzle in my identity search along the Dark Flight.

I Kissed A Girl (and Sorta Liked It)

As a typical middle-aged, business-owning woman—somewhat high pro-file, previously married for 10 years, mother of two children, gainer and loser of hundreds of pounds, kid-schlepper, high-powered deal broker, new-hair-color seeker (to stave off gray)—it's safe to say I've had a fantasy or two. When it comes to imagining what it would be like to be with another woman, I'm not alone.

Mark didn't know for years that during our third breakup I had a tryst with another woman. I'd like to believe I was the sort of woman with the decency to remember her name, but I don't. I've heard that women's desire to explore female physicality increases as they mature. Maybe we just want to know what it's like to be with a woman through the eyes of man. For me, it was more on the path of seeking identity. Perhaps these things, combined with loneliness, are why I found myself at Club Sesso, a swingers establishment belonging to Ron Jeremy, of porn flick fame.

After a sympathy invitation from a friend who knew I was down due to heartbreak, I was inconspicuously tucked into a corner, clutching a double shot of Patron. It was 9:45. Couples and singles filtered in, to a blaring Lady Gaga singing *Bad Romance*. My friend trotted off to catch up with the bartender. Theresa, a club volunteer, was scheduled to take me on an "orientation," to introduce the amenities and rules of the club. Hospitality from the staff thus far had been top notch, like a fancy hotel or classy restaurant.

My meager stance gave me away. Theresa walked up, extended a hand and warm smile, and introduced herself. I guessed her age at 40. She was neither stunning nor homely, both preconceived notions I'd imagined about people who'd come here. She revealed she was an ambulance driver, divorced, with two children aged 6 and 8. Then she added that instead of the perils of the "online thing," she comes here to have a safe, sexual social life.

Theresa seemed so *average* as she walked and talked about gang bang and naughty school girl party nights, like someone I'd chat with at my son's soccer games. Along the walls, jumbo TV screens emitted porn.

Upstairs were cube-shaped rooms with windows. Theresa said if I chose to "play," I would use these rooms. She said that keeping the curtains open so others could watch was optional, then added, "Just sanitize all the furniture when you're done," and pointed to large dispensers with sanitizing towels next to a box of colored condoms.

By the time we got to the twilight buffet area downstairs, Theresa explained that an extravagant meal of fruit, pancakes, cheeses, and cookies would be served after 11. The juxtaposition between normalcy and eroticism was palpable. I chuckled. *Go upstairs, have your brains fucked out by a stranger, then come on down for some good ol' fashioned pancakes.*

People started to arrive. There was an attractive couple in their mid-20s and I wondered if they were weirdos or freaks and whose idea it was to be here—his, hers, or both, and why they felt the need to come to a place like this.

I glanced over to Theresa, who offered an *I taught you everything you need to know* look and said, "We're here for safety. You have every right to say, 'no.' If you get a negative response, let us know," and pointed to the 250-pound bouncer standing firm near the bar.

I felt as if I was stepping off the tallest of ledges. I thanked Theresa and looked around at what had become a crowded room made up of couples, single women, a few men—and middle-aged, naive me. They all knew something I didn't.

The night started off with people dancing to Madonna, Daft Punk, Prince. A few girls were kissing, there was some harmless grinding, then, seamlessly things progressed to *we're not in Kansas anymore.* I forced myself out of a corner, a fresh blanco double in hand (I would be taking a cab home) and moved around the club to take all of it in.

People were in full swing, literally. In a room upstairs, the curtains were open and there was a voluptuous woman being worshipped by 5 guys. One rubbed her feet, another brushed her hair, one buff guy kissed her. Completing her harem was a gorgeously dark Hispanic man stroking her breasts, and a man with his face burrowed between her large, milky thighs. Unsure of where to fix my gaze, I landed on her contentment, her closed eyes; she was in the stratosphere. *So this—to feel free, be worshipped, uninhibited, adored—is why people come here?*

By the upstairs bar was a small group gathering for the S & M rope-tying demonstration. I couldn't reconcile the diversity of people I saw. They were fat and thin, old and young, black and white, couples and singles, and if not for this being a swingers club, the landscape would have resembled a Sunday outing to a farmers' market, sans kids in strollers. I wondered if they were lost souls, searching for meaning, or escape, or merely freedom? Or were they like the harem lady, seeking admiration just for a night?

Lost in thought, a sudden tap on the shoulder startled me. A pretty woman with chestnut hair and wide brown eyes stood there, smiling. To her side was a tall man, with salt and pepper hair and emerald eyes, who, I guessed by their matching rings, was her husband. "Hi," she said, "I'm (whatever her name was) and this is my husband, (whatever his name was). We saw you standing here and thought you might want company."

"Thank you," is all I could think to say. I qualified my awkwardness with, "This is my first time." They turned to each other, then smiled, as if they'd agreed to make a sizable donation to a favorite charity. The woman whose name I don't remember (we'll call her Jane) declared she understood. The husband (we'll call him Dick) offered to buy us a round of drinks.

While Dick was gone, I learned that Jane taught middle school. I didn't want to know where (in case it was at one of my kids' schools) and I tried to relax into normal conversation, as if I was at a networking event or party. Jane was witty. She was at home in her skin. She eloquently spoke about the lack of public school funding. I revealed nothing about myself. She wore a low-cut royal blue dress and I found myself thinking like a man—a first!—desiring to discreetly look down at her semi-exposed breasts.

Clearly Jane was attracted to me, and with exchanged flirtatious grins (if I could silence mental sneers of judgment), I could have crossed this off my fantasy to-do list. Dick came back, though, drinks in hand like party favors, and with a slight nod of approval acknowledged that Jane and I were having a good time. Jane emitted a seductive scent of jasmine and cherries.

After more idle chitchat, Jane leaned in to me and whispered, "Do you wanna play?" My cheeks flushed; I was turned on, nervous. Mark's face flashed in my mind. I remembered I was heartbroken. Guilt seeped in as if I was cheating, but then I recalled he had left.

I took Jane's hand and led her to a room. Dick followed. I asked for closed curtains. She was closer to me; the body beneath her tight dress was electric. Without hesitation, her soft lips planted squarely onto mine. A woman's kiss wasn't how I had imagined; it was softer, sweeter. Her hair felt silky in my hands. Decades of curiosity and Mark's rejection melted away. I thought of the heavyset goddess from the room next door—*Am I her?*

Jane's skin was a satiny ribbon. Her lips were gentle sea sponge. The way she handled me, with small, delicate hands, and the way I handled her reminded me of two butterflies flittering in unison toward the sun. Part of me transported out of body to enable my spirit to inhale. The other part was hot, charged, and alive. Dick wanted to join in, but I was not comfortable being with another man. That would have felt like cheating.

The next moments warped while I adored all of Jane's body. As I truly tasted her and she allowed, I watched as she lowered her wide brown eyes. She was reaching closer to that cosmic place, grabbing my hair. I wanted to transport her all the way to the spiral of the galaxy. Dick disappeared into the wall, it was just Jane, and with her heat came the fire of light and speed, of groaning, and she was there, in the infinite space and time where only momentary love from a stranger echoes in the silence of quivering skin.

My own breathlessness was beautiful and strange, as though I'd crossed a threshold.

Suddenly the urge to get up and leave overtook me like the collapse of a black hole. I was done with that scene and wanted to go home. I stood up, looked at Jane, then at Dick, clumsily apologized for the hasty departure, and pulled my dress on while heading out the playroom door.

I fled like Cinderella at the chime of midnight, down the stairs, past a video screen blaring porn, paused to notice the buffet food was out (it looked colorful and delicious!), crossed the crowded dance floor, past intertwining strangers, and found my way outside to the relief of the fresh midnight air. There was a taxi waiting in front. I got in and stared out the window the whole way home. I was empty and invigorated.

* * * * *

One early fall night a few weeks after Club Sesso, I was eating dinner with my kids and the phone rang. It was Mark. I was stunned to hear his voice. He asked if he could come over. My stomach churned. I wasn't sure this was a good idea after months into our third breakup without speaking. My pockets felt empty of trust tickets. Yet my heart dug in, and beneath buried lint, I found one more.

Twenty minutes later, he was at my door and proceeded to spend the next three days in nonstop apology and explanation. Was I cautious? Yes. Hesitant? Absolutely. In love? Eh, it was true.

After a few weeks of talking, two counseling sessions, and his intentional repair of the serious damage he'd done, Mark sold his house in Forest Grove and moved in with us. His integration back into my life was rocky. My kids had reason to doubt, my friends had reason to doubt. I was betting on faith and love.

A little over a year later, Mark proposed, a week after Terry had told me, "We're done." We got married with a small gathering at Cornelius

Pass Roadhouse in an old octagonal barn, on March 7, 2015. The wedding had been planned in only a few months; it was simple and gloriously fuss free.

* * * * *

The beginning of my marriage, the moment of committing to a forged relationship, coincided with the beginning of my Dark Flight. It was surreal to experience conflicting emotions. I was thrilled to commence the rest of our life as a union. Meanwhile, I, as an individual, started my aimless Flight into an identity abyss. How was I to be part of a "we" when I had nothing of "me"?

I had financial considerations from a pending lawsuit, fits and starts of piecing together an income through marketing consulting, plus everything that had happened to me, for me, and because of me. Logistically and emotionally, all of it had impacts.

Mark was amazing and supportive throughout the legal proceedings. He had stood beside me the whole time. And still the timing and circumstance yielded an inherent conundrum: How does one enter a dark time to search their own identity when they're partnered or married? I'm not saying being married makes a Dark Flight of the Self any harder or easier. I have no way of knowing a difference. But the internal question was always on my mind.

Unforeseen conflicts arose because at his core, Mark is a fixer. He solves problems. He gets frustrated if he can't. I don't blame his frustration in not being able to fix me. As months, and my identity crash, dragged on, *I* was sick of me. Because a Dark Flight is so deep and ethereal, it's difficult to describe what's wrong or offer insight into how or when things might change.

The conflict between being a "me" and "we" became apparent one morning when I took a walk. I noticed two ducks swimming in a pond.

They were closely paired as one paddled beside the other. I reflected on how my Dark Flight of the Self was also dragging along Mark. It's unfair that there are innocent bystanders caught in the wake. I had guilt over that, though it wasn't my fault, per se. Still, the unavoidable weight was there. I'd let him down. What was wrong with me?

I wondered how far a duck would stray if it wanted to swim upstream. What happened in a marriage when one half of a couple wanted familiar and the other wanted unknown? Hopes might be different and that can be painful to face. If it comes down to having different hopes, what then? Can two separate hopes coincide?

Waving the Stars
Shows the Stripes

I was already lost, trying to find a way within my Self and the marriage. We inherently have different ways of seeing the world and Mark was getting frustrated. He wanted to help and couldn't, wanted answers I couldn't give. Then came the barrel of fuel thrown on the fire: election day, November 8, 2016.

If you're a Trump supporter, skip over this section. It would be dandy if some of the book's other information offered inspiration, but I get it—these are divisive times. The 2016 election split millions of couples, families, friends, and colleagues across the country, and it prompted a huge rift between Mark and me. Disdain and/or support of 45 has torn apart relationships that will never heal.

Like thousands of others, Mark's vote for Trump was not a vote *for* Trump, it was *against* the system. It was a frustration vote against perceived corruption. It was a "Fuck you" to the man. He would have voted for Pee Wee Herman if he'd been on the ticket. But this explanation was not enough for a long time.

This information is not to out Mark or judge him, but the vote was a huge marital wedge for us. It added relationship confusion during an already confusing time for each of us individually, and threw in a big measure of social confusion. It just made even more of a mess out of wondering who I was in the world.

There was post-election proliferation of fear, which complicated the process of piecing back together my midlife identity. And if it was doing that to me, I guessed it was to others as well. How could I find who I was if, through unprecedented political realities, I could no longer count on social structures, personal rights, or promised liberties I had believed I could always count on? I love my country and what it's meant to represent.

Whether external structures merely felt like or actually were falling apart, the situation left no solid assurance. With a constant barrage of news and media related to politics, it was hard to not feel deflated.

* * * * *

Political labels today suck. They don't represent what they used to. I see a giant flag mounted on someone's car, flapping as it drives by and I glare at the driver. It bothers me that I now automatically associate the person who's waving it as proclaiming freedom to judge, divide, discriminate. Waving the stars and stripes has become a symbol for everything it's NOT.

I live in Portland, Oregon: a Democratically tipped city known for forward-thinking policies. It's also, I'll add, predominantly white. I grew up in Los Angeles, and in the neighborhood where I was raised, I was the minority. I was used to being in a melting pot of cultures, languages, ethnicities. "Other" was mainstream. I never felt unspoken tension about people different from me. It's become painfully obvious that in many parts of America, even in 2019, this is not the case.

Portland is a progressive geographic bubble within a conservative landscape. There are pockets of slightly diversified populations, yet nearly 85 percent of Oregon is white. That said, our circle of face-to-face friends is largely made up of Democrats and Independents, with a small handful of fiscally minded Republicans who contribute large chunks of time and money to a myriad of causes related to justice, homelessness, and equality. The current administration's chaotic modus operandi has placed many of our friends on high alert, lowered morale, and amped up engagement with a number of social crusades.

I will never forget election night, 2016.

That strange, surreal night.

Mark was downstairs in his man cave watching the returns. I opted not to watch; the constant media coverage was stressful. I didn't take for granted that Hillary Clinton would be the night's winner, although I was cautiously optimistic; plenty of people were divided after Bernie Sanders lost the Democratic bid. I just never comprehended that the people of America (whom I overestimated) would ever elect a television caricature so obviously neither suited nor qualified for presidency.

I knew Mark was anti-Clinton. Over the years he'd gathered, then reinforced, his "evidence" to form a strong opinion. I felt that several of his opinions were based more on repetitive rhetoric than on researched facts. Based on the election outcome, however, my thoughts on his thoughts make no difference.

What does make a difference is that on that night, as the country began to unravel, I didn't yet know what bubble he'd filled in on the ballot. When I woke up the next morning to a stark and bizarre reality, in shock over what the election result would potentially mean for America, my heart ached.

I don't recall the morning's interactions between Mark and me. I wanted to avoid him. Everywhere I went that day, people were walking around in a daze. Sentiments of mourning, shock, disgrace, and sadness were palpable. "Can you believe it?" must have been exchanged millions of times between friends, colleagues, and strangers.

When Mark came home from work that night, we sat at a quiet dinner table. We started to talk about the election, and then, mid-sentence, he mentioned something about his vote for Trump. I wasn't sure I'd heard correctly, but I knew I'd heard correctly.

"What?" I said, as I locked eyes with him.

He mumbled something like, "Anyone but her . . . " I didn't want to hear it.

Disbelief churned in my stomach, like I'd just found out he'd cheated on me. I no longer recognized the man I married. I dropped the fork and left the table in tears. That night I "slept" downstairs in the spare room. I was up all night contemplating how we'd go on.

I replayed the tape over and over in my mind that if he was anti-Hillary, he'd had three additional options other than voting *for* Trump: 1) Vote for one of the Independent candidates; 2) fill in the blank with the name "Bernie Sanders"; and 3) don't vote at all. To me, a vote *for* something is not a vote *against* something. A vote *for* something is what you stand for.

Mark saw his choice differently.

Over the years that followed, that event became a nearly insurmountable wedge. I held a lot of resentment. I couldn't fully forgive him.

I'm clear that Mark isn't happy with where things are politically now, a few years after his "Fuck you" vote. Perhaps in spite of his immense frustration over a broken system, he and many others couldn't have known, seen, or imagined what many had predicted and feared.

I can't comprehend why or how anyone would now support or stand by Trump or what he represents, given how this administration has performed—the threatened state of our democracy, attacks against journalists and a free press, dozens of legal investigations into financial malfeasance, voter fraud, election misconduct and collusion, willful destruction of diplomatic foreign relationships (which took decades to build), and reversals on policies designed for environmental, health, cultural, and educational protections.

There are some things about the 2016 election which are true and that I need to convey.

First, I need to clarify who Mark is:

Mark is hard-working, loyal, honest.

Mark is the one who will buy a sandwich for a homeless man he thinks is hungry.

Mark told me that if Bernie had been on the ticket, he would have voted for him.

Mark is not a small-minded zealot afraid of change.

Mark is not racist.

Mark doesn't hide behind religion as a means to discriminate.

Mark is the one you call for help to remove a downed tree.

Mark is the prepared one who packs matches, a knife, and toilet paper for a woods walk.

Mark is the one who always arrives 10 minutes early.

Mark is the one who believes that everyone should just do what's right.

Mark is the one who returns a shopping cart to where it belongs.

Mark is the one who will stay after a party to clean up.

I also need to explain how we got through the wedge. In order for us to move on, we had to spend hours in counseling unraveling (my) resentment. It had to be reaffirmed, over and over again, that his fundamental values as a person were initially what I believed. Every time I'd hear some awful news about some horrible policy act, I'd indirectly blame Mark. I seethed that he had contributed to getting us into the mess.

Every time we'd go to a party and politics came up, or people expressed frustration about the state of the world, I'd cringe. It's not something Mark hid intentionally, but considering our circle of friends, it's definitely not something he advertised. Only a few of my friends knew, because of the friction it had created.

It wasn't until two years later that I was able to ask if knowing what he did at that point, would he have voted differently. I didn't want to know the answer, but I had to know the answer. He said he would have voted differently.

Because of how charged the topic is, it's hard to explain how a "Fuck you" vote is just that, and doesn't define the person who cast it. There are millions of people going through this divisive struggle and what he and I went through as a couple is symbolic of a national debate. Even though it's hard for me to find justification, I believe it's important to separate those who voted and remain in *support* of 45 from those who voted *against* the system. I don't believe these voters are coming from the same place.

How can we find compassion in such intense times?

Unfortunately, the social, cultural, and economic ramifications we're witnessing go beyond frustration with a broken system. They go beyond religious zeal, although there's plenty of that to hide behind. This penetrates to the core of deeply rooted racism. Positions of power have been obtained by instilling fear. The complicated layering of our country's disparate beliefs, troubles, inequities, and hopes are buried beneath a blanket of prevailing privilege. Those with it can't see it, don't want to relinquish it, and sure as hell are not going to admit it.

Add in a deluge of social media, constant reminders of division, an endless stream of news and non-news—no wonder people are depressed, isolated, defeated. These past few years have worn us out. In the days after the election, I felt lucky when I found the energy to brush my teeth. Finding my new midlife Self in the wake of fear and daily Armageddon? Yeah, right.

Everything Is Political

I'm on a plane heading to Las Vegas. My headphones are on. Whitney Houston is serenading me. I'm reading a book called *The Possibility of Everything*, written by my writing coach, Hope Edelman. It's a kick-ass book. Her words are funny. Poignant.

I'm squeezed in the middle seat between two burly men (one's my husband), like a wedge of iceberg lettuce between thick slices of crusty bread. The flight attendant delivers a bag of peanuts. She resembles Sandra Bullock. Mark is sleeping next to me and is man-spreading his legs. Anytime we go somewhere that involves side-by-side seating, I get a paltry third of the leg space compared to the two-thirds his frog sprawl commands. Through the portal of a potato-shaped window, I see scattered clouds of pale whipped butter spread over beige tapestries.

A woman in the row across from us is large. She has two seats. My heart breaks a little that we live in a world where a person has to face humiliation on a daily basis from being extremely overweight, especially when flying. She's paid the price of two even though she's only one. I'm not sure what the equitable thing to do would be from a business stand-point. She's a single person that requires two seats, yet each seat has a value to the airline as a company needing to balance the books.

The thought leads me to an important question: How can we cohabitate in a world where neither side is wrong and, more to the point, both sides are right? Given that there are many increasingly divisive opinions related to people's rights of dignity, economic safety, and diversity in voice, there's a growing aversion to discourse. We're getting better at creating taller, more elaborate social fences.

I'd had a recent conversation with a friend and he said something many fear: "I don't see how we're going to get out of this." I understood: only a few years ago, many of today's worries were not on our radar. Nuclear war, financial collapse from gross wealth disparity, irreparable devastation to the environment, the dismantling of our educational system, the rolling back of rights protecting women's bodies, women's choices, and women's equality—all are back in a state of play.

How much will be destroyed?

How fragile are our checks and balances?

Where are reason and sanity and equity and justice?

How much do we not know?

I'm scared. I'm scared for the world my children are inheriting.

A country of violence makes me afraid. Sometimes when I drop my son off at school, for a brief moment I worry about his safety. *Is this the day a shooter shows up and blows holes in classrooms?* Mornings when I'm at the gym naked and vulnerable in the shower, the image of a loose gunman popping rounds crosses my mind and I imagine the escape route I'd use. I feel less safe these days in crowded places such as outdoor concerts or the mall. It's not that I live my life in fear, it's just weird and sad that these thoughts unintentionally cross my mind at all.

Internal midlife identity struggles and trying to reconcile a place for my Self in an uncertain world make me anxious, riddled with disbelief, angry and asking questions I never thought I'd be asking. This is where I get midlife rage, although there's nowhere to put it in daily life. This is where I get that people just want to tear shit up. This is where I get moments when I want to scream as loud as my vocal cords will stretch, until they are raw and on fire. This is where I want to slam glass plates to the ground and crash through walls like a green gamma-ray-laden Hulk— to recklessly expel all the pent-up angst that politely hovers beneath the surface until the surface can no longer withstand the pressure and BAM!!! it all explodes into fragments of fed-up release.

I can't comprehend the anger or worry of others on the social edge. Immigrants. People of color. People in poverty. Journalists working to preserve democracy. Veterans. Those who are sick and in need of health care. Senior citizens. People with mental health issues or drug addictions. Women. Those who love someone of the same sex. Residents of Puerto Rico, who survived the hurricane and need more than paper towels thrown at them. Those who believe in facts. Those who know the Earth is round.

I have friends from different racial backgrounds who have said that the racism is nothing new. It's always been here. As a straight, middle-aged white women with Jewish and Mexican heritage, I can't begin to understand the challenges for a person of another race or culture. Perhaps with all that's transpired in the last few years, there's something on a grander anthropological human scale: we're in the midst of a vast, dark, dramatic swing in order to eventually balance out. A stark contrast might be what's needed to find our way to justice. To light. To true democracy. But at the expense of how many people's safety, dignity, and equality?

On the home front, do politics matter in marriage? Can differing values add broader understanding, or will they produce constant conflict? No one person will ever mirror our philosophies, our intellect, our emotional embodiments, our values.

Is marriage meant to fulfill these aspects of our lives, or to be more of a practicality, as in the old days of farmers and women who married for joint survival? You know, to have someone to wipe our ass when we're 80?

I was so confused.

At that point, as I navigated my beliefs and identity, I was becoming more adrift within my marriage. How could I become a fully realized individual within the context of a committed relationship—in other words, circumvent the identity of a "we" to allow the unstoppable advancement of a "me"?

I glanced over at Mark, who was awakening over the Nevada desert as we started the descent into Las Vegas.

I couldn't change him. Mark was who he was. Yet, I was not who I was . . . was I?

My Mirror/My Self

In my previous fantasies of an alternate life, with an alternate pant size and an alternate lover (the hipster bearded guy with blue eyes at the bank, the dapper grocery clerk with pencil jeans beneath a green apron), sometimes my mind would drift in Harlequin-worthy narratives . . .

She'd imagined a more vibrant man. A man who liked Pop-Tarts in bed, someone on the edge who snuck Swedish fish into a movie theater and stuffed a few cinnamon bombs into his mouth on the heels of buttered popcorn. As she scanned the curve of his chin, imagining her index finger tracing the firm outline, she thought maybe he could have been a man that once ate Hostess cherry pies, a naughty boy pulling out the forbidden pleasure slick from its sealed holster, the gooey red fruit protected by a glaze-covered crust. The thought of his innocent pleasure reveling in the sugar and crust and dripping fruit made her thighs vibrate. She purred with desire and murmured a breathless question about the food he craved most, until the fantasy bubble made a loud POP! at his reply of "hummus . . ."

Even in the imperfect world of internal Harlequin narrations, I was thinking about how life might've been different with someone else. Someone wealthy. Someone with numerous college degrees. A friend once told me that one person or marriage isn't supposed to satisfy everything. She said the problem was clearly my expectations; if I wanted to be truly happy, I needed to recalibrate those expectations.

I thought about the feasibility of resetting one's relationship clock. How realistic was that? To go back to a time or place and somehow start over. How can you erase everything you've done, everything you've been through, everything you already know that you can't *not* know about someone?

I felt guilty. The problem must have been me, because I was the one who had a problem. I was the one searching, the one disappointed, the one whose expectations never quite aligned with reality.

I would have loved to be a more a fascinating wife. The Amal Clooney of beauty, confidence, accomplishment, grace. I wondered how Mark saw me, if he thought, *Wow I hardly recognize her.* Did he want an easier wife? Somebody who wore big hoop earrings and dangly bracelets, smelled like peaches and smiled like whipped cream?

* * * * *

Things got complicated between us when it was hard to discern from where our conflicts derived. Differences in who we were as individuals? My identity grief and subsequent depression? Weight gain by both of us? My perimenopausal hormone fluxes? Or just reaching that stage in all relationships when couples faced challenges?

I was head over heels in love with Mark for six solid years. We were the couple that made people sick. We had easy connection. Physical contact was never a problem. Our sex life was healthy. We wanted each other most of the time.

But now we weren't connecting emotionally, and intimacy was hard to muster. I felt distant. I couldn't explain what was going on emotionally and Mark couldn't fix it. I was depressed, tired, fat, and uninterested. Because we weren't making connections in emotional ways, I had little motivation to connect in physical ones.

This was topped off by the fact that we'd both gained weight. I had added 45 pounds. Him? I'm not sure how many pounds he'd put on, but he wasn't the picture of health he'd once been. If we'd both taken care of our health, would that have maintained desire? Did the fact we were less intimate in turn cause waning desire? In other words, when you do it less, do you want it less?

When I'm not physical with my partner, it's hard to connect emotionally. When I don't connect emotionally, there's no desire for the physical. I was lonely most of the time. Mark and I lived like roommates. I was going through so much inside, and my stuff became a confused midlife fusion of identity change, hormone swings, and depression. I couldn't discern which was what. Mark was stuck living with an emotional anvil.

I couldn't force myself to feel connected, nor could I fake it till I made it. I never truly considered divorce, although I did imagine a life on my own. I knew I loved Mark, but we were at a crossroads, whether I'd caused it or not. I didn't see a way out. I asked myself a hard question: *Do I want to find my way back?* Having an honest answer could help forge a direction toward something, because we were hanging on.

I realized I did.

From that answer, I knew we had to get to the bottom of issues that kept reappearing. Acknowledgment of the physical disconnect was a place to start.

* * * * *

I often wondered if men know what it's like to disconnect from their bodies. I've felt disconnected from my body and have had sex when I wasn't in the mood out of obligation and to avoid feeling like a failure as a wife. This thought floated in my mind when we got into bed one night. I was clothed, wearing a sweatshirt and leggings. Mark wanted to have sex and I didn't want to let him down . . . again.

I lay there, frigid on the inside, eyes shut tight, unable to look into his eyes, mad at myself for being so far away, unable to participate in a spousal way. When the moment was done, I kept my eyes shut tight, feeling empty and guilty and faraway from him and my body, and us, until the tears rolled down to remind me we were there, alone together.

* * * * *

The menopause metaphor of a changing season is poetic and gentle. It implies we just glide on in from the summer of our lives into fall. The romanticized ideal of menopause—that we enter into a club of wise, silver-haired savants glowing with inner peace—is almost as disheartening as menopause itself. Even having "pause" as part of the word is misleading. Not one thing takes a break.

So *unlike* the seamless, untraceable nature of one season slipping into the next, there are instead never-ending surprises: pounds gained, bi-weekly periods, waking up in a cold pool of sweat, disappearing sexual desire, continual exhaustion, and physical reminders that life is half over. Hormonal deviations overshadowed a Me I once knew—the one with reliable periods that didn't require triple-stashing emergency tampons in the car, purse, and travel bag; a Me that once felt like a viable, desirable expression of womanhood who now wore sweatpants every day.

In terms of desire, it was like a damned light switch had been turned off. One day I woke up completely uninterested in sex. I knew it wasn't only us, or him, or lack of energy. How did I know it was hormones? I had zero desire. (If I had no interest in sex with him, yet found myself always taking care of myself, I'd know differently.)

I mourned the loss of raging chemistry, hunger, urgency, desperation, bewildered butterflies, sexual tension, insurmountable desire, unquenchable thirst, panicked longing.

No one would ever want me that way again.

* * * * *

Sex is fundamental in a relationship. I felt trapped because I didn't think keeping Mark happy should be a responsibility while I was going through what I was going through. I couldn't just push the desire button. Why is there such an unspoken expectation that women are the ones responsible for keeping their partners physically pleasured? And the assumption that if they don't, their partners will run off to get sex elsewhere? I worried and felt guilty about this all the time. I felt like a failure as a wife and a woman.

If I exercised, took multivitamins, Omega 3s, calcium, iron, and other supplements, would that increase my vitality and sex drive? Do women come back from the dark sides of their moons? I wanted to figure out how much of my lack of desire was hormonal or depression, but I was overwhelmed by the amount of information on both. I also wondered how much of my lack of desire was because Mark wasn't putting forth any effort. Women appreciate little things. We need to know we're not taken for granted. We need to hear that we're appreciated in a love language *we* speak. I got that Mark fixed the sink and installed flooring in our house. Those acts were *his* love language, but sometimes I wanted to feel special in a girly love language sort of way.

* * * * *

After weeks of having no energy night after night, one Friday afternoon I forced myself to go to the gym. Afterwards, I felt replenished. Since I had more energy than I'd had in a long time, I called Mark to see when he'd be home and asked if he wanted to go do something. Mark got home 30 minutes later. We went to the mall. I was surprised by how bouncy I felt. I even thought about the possibility of sex. Everything went well at the mall, we enjoyed each other's company. We went home and things were conversational and easy. I felt a familiar spark and connection.

As we settled into bed, both perusing our laptops, Mark started listening to a video about the issue around Hillary Clinton's emails. It was loud and the whole incident set me back. If I'd had a boner, playing a politically related video would have been classified as a "boner-killer." But he didn't know I'd been in the mood. He couldn't read my mind and he was sure as shit unable to read my sporadic, half-hearted, mostly comatose body language.

The missed opportunity was not his fault. I had a whole separate world of thought and expectation. And just like that, we were back to a divide.

A lot got lost in translation with us.

* * * * *

Mark initially had resistance to counseling. It wasn't something to which he'd been exposed. But after he'd left me multiple times the first few years, during his identity meltdown, he agreed to give it a try. I'd already been seeing Raphael for a while and had respect for his clarity and insight. I thought Mark would like him.

Mark and I started going as a couple. Sometimes our communication was so stalled it felt like a giant unscalable wall. But Raphael broke down the wall brick by brick and found ideas and language that translated to us both. Mark has a self-reliant nature, so seeking help isn't something that comes naturally to him. But he recognized counseling's impact and every time we went, he admitted he'd gotten something of value.

One session in particular made a big difference. Raphael spent the session diffusing a heated battle of mutual, long-standing resentment. As much as I was lost and disconnected, Mark felt the same. As we went back and forth, spewing anger as Raphael refereed, he whittled it down and whittled it down, comment by comment, until the truth of the hurt was unburied. I felt unheard. Mark felt disrespected.

Over the months I'd felt adrift in marriage, I'd questioned if we were *too* different from one another. But once we'd battled it out, we discovered it wasn't *what* we weren't connecting about, it was *how* we weren't connecting.

The realization was substantial: we had two faulty toolboxes, not two faulty people. This took a burden off my shoulders and left possibility. We were inept at communicating. Our *how* was fucked up.

This idea may be basic, but during that session the answers for how to reconnect became clearer. Our communication capacity was key for everything—how we related, how we became intimate, how we helped one another, how we provided space to each other, how we understood a not-so-far-apart political landscape, how we solved resentments, how we raised our kids, how we dealt with finances . . . all of it.

I suspect many couples struggle with coming together, growing apart, and coming together again. It seems like this would be an organic process. We committed to guided efforts in counseling to explore making the *how* better. We're still committed and still in counseling, but I'm optimistic.

I love my husband. He's part of my everything.

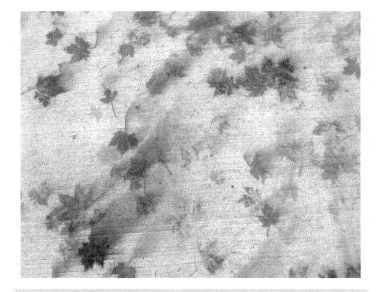

Never Gonna Have
It All at Once

There's always something to work on. We're never going to have all our shit together at once. By this, I mean having the love of our life, our health, our youth, a great job, a bank account fat with savings, spiritual enlightenment, an ideal weight, and accolades from throngs of admirers. Whatever it is you want or I want, the long-ass list of human desires, eh... probably never going to have it all. At least, not at the same time.

Physical upkeep is a fair metaphor. Will I ever have, simultaneously, no gray roots, shaved legs, shaved armpits, coifed love zone, no mustache, manicured eyebrows, painted toenails, manicured hands, and my ideal weight of 150 pounds? Nah. It's not going to happen. Variations are endless. Good weight, bad hair. Bad weight, coifed muff. Pedicured toenails, sprouting upper lip.

I have never had the expectation that I would have it all. I didn't go through an internal pressure cooker over the external appearances of my life. Having a high-powered job wasn't paramount, although when I had one, I enjoyed it. Making money hasn't been a primary track, but even being self-employed, I've been able to get by.

These days, I apply all the editorial, operations, and production skills I acquired as a magazine publisher to create publications for universities and large companies. I can do it more efficiently than their marketing departments and produce a more professional product. I also consult with companies on how to best tell their most valuable stories. Many ask me to write their company narratives, mission statements, and blog content.

Although work stuff stays consistent as I meander into more of who I am apart from what I do, I'm shifting away from writing other people's stories and into sharing my own. Yes, the idea is as scary as Freddy Krueger at a balloon-twisting competition. However, I want to continue speaking to book clubs, professional groups, women's associations, and conferences about the often not-talked-about notion of midlife identity grief. This is such a tender and surreal time. Nearly everyone I know has gone through some personal and/or professional variation of the Flight. I believe I can help.

One thing that identity loss reiterated for me was that friendships became even more important. Having good friends to connect with when I felt so disconnected was an anchor. But let's be real. Friendships change in midlife. Many people are in the middle of something that they really don't understand. (I love you, Paul McCartney!) Even though some travel or are busy with work or kids, these are not the culprits for revolving doors of friendship.

It's as if a large layer of identity gets shed, and with it go the no-longer-compatible friendships associated with that layer. Could be a layer related to the person you were at one time, or a layer that signified a job you had or a town where you once lived. No matter. It's as if the Dark Flight of the Self does the friendship vetting for you.

By the end of my Dark Flight, friends I'd known for years were no longer part of my life. On the individual level, these losses were hurtful and confusing. On the macro level, the friendships had run their course. Even though I couldn't find logical explanations at the time, it makes sense now as I look back. If we're no longer who we once were, it would stand to reason that we'd need an updated friends list to reflect who we're becoming.

Just as I lost some friends, I also made new ones. Friends who became supportive in surprisingly different ways than the friends I'd had before; people who were creative in a broader range of talents and skills. It was as if the emergence of my Self had a whole new hall of mirrors to reflect upon and extend the reach of my searching wings.

Many people I knew were lonely; it was palpable. The advent of social media enhanced illusions of how connected life was *supposed* to feel and accentuated isolation. Perhaps this is why people in midlife act out in attempts to fill empty holes of loneliness: to invoke a sense of something—anything—tangible.

I also realized that what had stayed the same throughout my life were the things I'd wanted: to feel an inner acceptance of and honest connection to my Self. To feel emotions and not hide behind thoughts or expectations. To not disassociate from experiences.

I was still cognitively living my life; I experienced the world through thoughts, ideas, opinions, judgments, conflicts, and assessments.

I could always tell you what I *thought.*

I could almost never tell you how I *felt.*

When I participated in meditation group exercises over the years and was asked to feel my legs "sitting on a chair, touching the floor," I had to feign acknowledgment.

Instructor: "What inside sensations are you experiencing at this moment?"

Me: "Uh, fuck if I know."

I contemplated how many people could do this—identify bodily sensations or emotions. What was wrong with me that I couldn't? Feeling out of touch with my inner Self and unable to connect was so frustrating. It seemed many people had the secret handshake or capacity for this experience, and I was perpetually on the sideline *thinking* about my life, analyzing my life, intellectualizing my life, while others actually lived theirs.

* * * * *

Motherhood: Midlife's Ultimate Matrix

Despite an existence that was primarily defined by thinking and thoughts, one aspect of my life that never failed to directly tap into my emotions was being a mother. At the same time, nothing kicked midlife surrealism in the ass quite like motherhood. I had two kids, aged 11 and 15, when my Dark Flight started. Although I wasn't able to cook wholesome meals or stay up at night and play board games, I couldn't totally fall apart. I still had to guide, oversee, and support my children.

I feel guilty for all the times I checked out, but I was barely hanging on. I wanted the escape a couple of drinks—usually whiskey—and a couple of tokes gave me. There was a point when I worried Mark would worry about the drinking, but I never felt I was on a slippery slope. In fact, I was clear I wasn't. Even though I drank every night, it was never more than two drinks, and never to get drunk, but to smooth the edginess of feeling so lost. I'm not proud that's how I got through, but we do what we have to. The nightly drinking and toking ended on its own sometime in the middle of the Dark Flight.

Something that I will probably never lose from the Dark Flight period is my guilt over not being totally present for my kids and feeling like a failure as a mother. I could have, should have, done more, been more, given more. They weren't aware of how deep my isolation was. I kept it from them, but they're perceptive. They were aware of what transpired with my business sale and lawsuit, that I'd been cheated out of what I earned.

I didn't want to unload onto them what I was going through because one, I myself didn't fully understand what was happening, and two, I didn't want them to worry I was going to fall apart. I tried to strike a balance between being real about where I was (they were old enough to understand), without the weight or extent of my struggles.

I was already letting myself down. I was absent from Mark and felt guilty about that. I didn't want my kids to be a casualty, too. Toward the end of the isolation, to make up for the guilt I felt about my failures from the front end of my Dark Flight, whenever they came into my room at night and wanted to talk, I stopped what I was doing to engage. When my daughter Violet came home at night from her job at Craft Warehouse, I was the first person she came to see. We sat, hung out, petted our beautiful black cat Leo, and talked. I wanted to always be available.

Yet all the relationship bedrock I'd spent years constructing between Violet and me and Ethan and me felt like illusions. The biggest holes in my heart, the most irreconcilable identity grief I felt came from shifting dynamics with my kids.

I believed that if I kept communicating, if I treated them with respect, encouraged their talents, and supported their interests, those tenets of motherhood would carry us through the inevitable teenage storms. But when adolescent separation happened for both of them, our relationships became a cluster of identity shape-shifting. Kids go through what they go through—rebellion, distancing, blaming—and for me, in the state I was in, it was an added precipice of identity loss and confusion.

Sometimes they no longer needed or wanted me. I became the odd elbow propped on a bed that could never find a comfortable spot, no matter where my body shifted, trying not to be in the way. Both kids pushed me further aside in their own ways, for their own reasons, and according to their own timelines. With Ethan, it started when he was 14, and for Violet it came at 18. Yet their individuations corresponded with each other's and in the midst of my midlife identity spiral.

Kids may grow and change but a mother is still the mother.

I did the math: an 18-year-old has lived for 157,680 hours. The parent was thinking of their child at least 95 percent of that time. (The remaining 5 percent transpires while we're asleep or nestled on a toilet). The 95 percent equals 141,912 hours of the parent's life (not to mention an additional nine months before children are even born). We can't just turn off that thinking pattern that's been forming for hundreds of thousands of hours.

As soon as they decide to push you away—whether it's at 14, or 16, or 18—they do so without warning. You just wake up one day and things between you and your child have changed. Somehow, overnight, an entirely new 3,287-page child-parent agreement had been drafted, signed, notarized, and served, and all you did was go to sleep the night before.

One of the hardest parts of being on the receiving end of these new agreements is that no matter what terms have been proclaimed—that you will be ignored, be made to feel irrelevant, become the source of all blame, and merely serve as a bank account or set of car keys—you as the parent are just supposed to take it. That's part of the new contract, too. (Whatever you do, DON'T read *The Giving Tree* as an adult. I made that mistake and cried for three days.)

I struggled with how to be a mother as well as a middle-aged woman weathering my own individual losses and identity changes—all while pasting on a Betty Crocker face that everything was well. This was a challenge I never figured out. All those years of mixed how-to-parent messages collided. "Never allow your personal trials to be seen by your kid because you don't want them to internalize or feel responsible for it" versus "Kids should see the authentic struggles a parent goes through. They need to understand that stressful events happen and it's how we handle these things that matters."

Breaking news, kids: mothers are not mannequins, absent of flaws and imperfections and fears and disappointments. We do our best but sadly, we lug around a bag of guilt bricks daily.

We hope and pray you'll love us anyway.

* * * * *

One specific way I tried to build and maintain a relationship safety net with my children was to take them traveling as they were growing up. I took Violet on her own and Ethan on his own for individualized experiences and attention. Sometimes I brought them both.

Traveling with my kids was a huge priority. As a child, I never went anywhere with my mom or dad. My dad was a world traveler and although he'd taken his stepdaughter many places, he had never taken me on a trip with him. I felt completely left out. My grandparents took my brother and me on small weekend trips to Balboa beach or Big Bear, but that was it. As a mom, I vowed that traveling with my kids would be our thing.

I deeply believed that showing them the world and sharing travel experiences would be a basis for true connection and common reference. No matter life's twists, turns, curve balls, or unexpected occurrences, we would always have memories from time spent in San Francisco or Maui or Amsterdam. When I owned the magazine, I could do this easily because I got press considerations. When that well dried up, I sometimes maxed out credit cards. It was that vital to me. Shared travel is life's most sacred experience. I know that throughout my kids' lives, they will have memories of those experiences we shared—of places and people and adventures—as the foundation of our bond.

Violet moved out the summer of 2018. She had turned 18 and wanted a change of scenery (which I get). She couldn't afford to live by herself, so she went to live with her father, 15 minutes away. I felt both comfort and resentment over this decision. I was happy she'd have somewhere safe to land while she figured out her life (at that time she had enrolled in community college and had a part-time job), yet even though my logic was unreasonable, it felt unfair that after raising Violet, her father got to enjoy her presence as a budding adult. I loved having my daughter around. Her presence was grounding and I loved who she was as a person. Even if she hadn't been my daughter, she'd still have been one of my favorite people. Not having her at home created a tremendous empty space in my heart and I struggled with the notion of holding on while letting go.

I experienced all kinds of relationship/motherhood/identity grief for months. I missed having her come home after work, sit on my bed, and tell me about her day. I missed taking random trips with her to Home Goods to casually peruse the aisles. I missed making her grilled cheese sandwiches when she was hungry. I missed seeing her in the morning, bundled up like a burrito in her covers, surrounded by stuffed animals and petting our cat Leo. I missed her excitement when she would show me a beautiful drawing as soon as she'd completed it. There were so many seemingly small yet profound honors of being her mom that unfolded on a daily basis. I missed them and her deeply.

Around this time, she took official measures to change her name to Taylor. At her job and for her school registration, Violet wanted to publicly be known as Taylor. She was working at Craft Warehouse and Starbuck's—both places where she dealt with the public—and she explained that she wanted to separate her personal and public selves.

While I respected Violet's desire to be called something else, this specific issue became another form of identity separation. To me, the person who had given birth to her, chosen her name, used her name for 18 years, Violet and her name were part of me. I couldn't bring myself to call her Taylor. It wasn't out of disrespect for her wishes or an intention to exert ego. Her name was a connection to her essence and that was a tremendous part of motherhood.

My crumbling identity and subsequent heartbreak over the shifting tide with my daughter took an even darker turn. There was a disagreement between her father and me over child support. Violet was unhappy that I pursued resolving the situation. A chain reaction of assumptions, misunderstandings, and projections was set off, prompting Violet to stop talking to me. She temporarily cut me out of her life.

I'd been completely convinced that no matter what happened in life, or between us, our relationship was solid enough to withstand any storms. That we had carefully constructed a labyrinth based on mutual trust, respect, and love. I was proud of who we were as mother and daughter. But now I'd been shut out.

I did everything I could: texted, wrote a letter, emailed, Facebook messengered, went to her work (that didn't go well), begged, pleaded, and cried. In the end, she said she didn't want to speak to me. It took the motherhood heartbreak to a whole other stratosphere. Every day, I thought about her. I missed her so much I ached. Sadly, and almost as a visual metaphor for the pain, the beautiful deep blue betta fish Violet had given me for Christmas four years earlier got sick. We had lots of snow that year, so I'd named him Snowflake. He'd become a loyal and comforting office companion.

Snowflake was like a dog; every time I went over to the tank to say hello, he'd excitedly swim up to me and wag his fins and tail. I've never seen a fish react as petlike. Snowflake actually knew who I was (he didn't do this for anyone else) and I attributed the connection between this little fish and me to the love with which he'd been given. It made Violet so happy to give him to me. Every time I gazed at Snowflake, I felt Violet and her love.

When Snowflake started to get sick, he struggled to swim to the top of the tank to greet me. He'd try and try to wiggle his fins and tail and muster the strength to paddle to the top, but halfway up, he would exhaust the minuscule energy he had. Defeated, he sank back down to the bottom. As the days passed, he was less able to paddle for as long or as high and eventually he just sat on the bottom of the tank, in the corner.

I wished there was something I could do to stop his suffering. I researched humane ways to end a fish's life (he was still alive and flushing was not humane) and there were none I had the will to execute. Plus, I had such guilt. I could never have *intentionally* killed Snowflake—he was a gift from my daughter. The three weeks he was half-alive were disconcerting.

When Snowflake finally died, my initial reaction was that I was a failure. Then an immense grief wave hit, because I hate it when things die and that beautiful fish brought such joy. I wished I could call Violet to share that her gift, our shared friend, was gone. I wanted it all back: her in my life, our unconditional, uncomplicated love, our innocence as mother and daughter.

My birthday fell on Mother's Day that year, a doubleheader, and I heard nothing from Violet. No recognition. No acknowledgment. All day I was depressed, missing my daughter, wondering how I had become so unimportant, not only as a mom, but as a person in her life.

Many friends stated that this happens. Sometimes kids just need their space, not to worry, that she'd come back around. And maybe on a developmental level, these situations happen between parents and children. It's complicated. I've been a child of a parent and a parent of a child. There are indeed two sides. Kids learn things, see things, need to discover things, make sense of things, or come to their own realization of things. They hold anger, resentment and build a novel of stories about how parents have fucked it all up. On a heart level, I get it.

We were missing out on each other's moments, though, moments big and small that could never be reproduced. If, heaven forbid, something happened to one of us, the disconnect would forever be cemented.

As a mother who loves her daughter more than life itself, the thought of infinite separation slayed me.

And part of me was angry at how useless and inconsequential I'd been left to feel. As the parent, we are supposed to be unconditionally understanding of our children's cycles. We are not supposed to have our own human feelings on matters of loss, anger or even disappointment. But as a person, being treated this way is painful. How is it that as the mother, you're the source of your child's pain and confusion, *and*, as the parent, are also helpless to do anything to make them feel better? This conundrum is heartbreaking.

You Have A Mother

you have a mother

who embodied your first breath for life

you have a mother

whose heart fused from steel to glass

once she held you

you have a mother

who never knew love's roundness

until touching your tiniest corners

you have a mother

with exposed fragile edges

you have a mother

dressed in cells plump with

thoughts and dreams and fears

you have a mother

who mingles with clouds

while carrying rocks

you have a mother

who wanders emptied midnight streets

in search,

in search

you have a mother

who carries a prayer candle in a windstorm

toward a gothic cathedral of love

it's a resilient flame we mothers carry

because our blood tells us so

we arrive to marvel how holy light penetrates

flawed yet beautiful

fragments of collaged stained glass

beneath the towering stone pillars

where lost mothers weep

to deliver an offering—a flicker of warmth

to find your way home

to find your way home

* * * * *

I've often wondered how many parents of my generation worked at keeping our kids "comfortable." Because we love so much and want to protect so fiercely, we intervene at all those tiny little junctures when our kids may face discomfort. A few examples: not letting them play in the rain because they might get wet, or not enforcing dish duty if they come home tired from school.

Frantically throwing down a towel ahead of them at every turn so they never have to step in the mud may not be the best thing. Can we later forgive ourselves for not teaching our children how to navigate discomfort and adversity with resilience? In trying to help, do we end up hurting? In trying to cushion, do we put off the fall? When our kids eventually fall, will it be harder and potentially cause more harm because the self-accountability stakes are higher?

When my son Ethan was around 10, he started playing video games. I had very strong opinions against having an Xbox at home. But between Ethan's father's home and Mark's own desire to have one around, I lost this battle. I believe video games are poison for a blossoming child's imagination. They breed complacency, desensitization, shortened attention spans, screen addiction, and anxiety in kids. Today's games are intentionally designed to be virtual drugs.

Ethan is one of the most compassionate, empathetic kids I know. Such a sweet and loving soul, since birth. The idea of his little innocent cells being infiltrated with such graphically subsidized violence never sat well with me. As a mother, I faced all the social battles I'd eventually lose when it came to protecting my son. There was a difference between the protection to keep him comfortable and the protections against unhealthy social currents of violence and sexualization at the core of video games.

When I've shared this belief, I've heard the protests (mostly from men), "Well, we had video games when we were kids," and I call bullshit.

We had Pong or had to walk to a 7-Eleven with a ziplock bag full of stolen quarters from our parents' change jar to play Defender or Asteroids. Never did we have eight-hour marathons, like zombies in front of screens blowing shit up.

Without trying to sound like an old man standing on a lawn yelling at clouds and waving a cane in the air, I believe the techno influence kids are under today has numbed if not sedated the cultivation of three very important Rs: Resilience, Resourcefulness, and Reflection. Resilience to engage and endure when challenges arise with peers, parents, employers, or self. Resourcefulness to creatively troubleshoot solutions to daily problems. Reflection on what's happening in the bigger world, above and away from a screen, and to internalize what gives deeper meaning to our lives.

To bring this back to my Dark Flight of the Self, when I was in the throes of real emotional struggle I needed to work when I could, which meant sometimes my kids were left to their own devices. Ethan would be on the Xbox for hours. It was a babysitter and I knew it, even though I hated the fucking thing. What was strange was that he'd be online with some of his friends, and they were on just as long as he was, and I realized their mothers knew it, too, and probably felt just as bad as I did. Just as inadequate. Just as guilty. I had allowed the contamination of his pure, unencumbered imagination and the slow sequestering of his creative potential. I got swept up in the tidal wave without even a flotation device to save us.

I had an amazing reminder, however, about the importance of the other things we mothers teach our children. When Ethan was 14, he and I were at a restaurant. I was upset at him because right before we left, I'd checked his grades online and several recurring complaints from teachers were noted. Missing assignments. Homework not turned in. I was frustrated with this habitual problem.

I'm sure Ethan felt bad about himself and my constant nagging. I didn't want to always be on his ass. But where was the self-accountability? I'd say that overall, I haven't been a pushover. I think I've been fair. I treat him like a young adult with respect and directness. Ethan knows where he stands.

So we're at this restaurant and this older lady comes up to me and tells me how impressed she was at how sweet and thoughtful Ethan was. It seems that earlier that morning, she'd witnessed him helping an older gentleman. She was quite emotional.

That's when I realized what matters. A kid can eventually learn better study habits or self-discipline, but you can't teach him to have a caring heart or genuine compassion. You can't teach him to have a soul. I felt so fortunate that Ethan's capacity for kindness was so clearly evident to the world, to a stranger in fact, and that she was deeply touched by witnessing his generous act. I will never forget that moment.

The timing was good, because I would soon need that moment to hold onto. One day I looked at Ethan and suddenly, as if out of nowhere, he was looking at me eye to eye. The change in him, in us, in our relationship, was happening so rapidly. The boy was becoming less of my boy and more of his own young evolving-man. The safety of a preadolescent cocoon had been torn by how deep his voice had become. All the bright naivete I had held about us as a mother and son started to tarnish. I felt his intentional separateness. Through a lower voice and taller stance he was being more and more exposed to the world I could no longer shield him from.

Had I taught him enough about treating women with respect? Respecting himself? How to stand up to injustice? How to protect himself from harm's way regarding drugs and the consequences of sex? Young boys are so impressionable. I held out on getting him a smart phone. He only had a flip phone until he was 14. Then it was his sister who got him an iPhone. I lost that battle, too, and it didn't take long for the new device to seduce him into oblivion. Games. Snapchat. Texts. Videos. He was like an addict, clutching the device tightly, unable to break free from the screen spell and engage with the world during car rides, restaurant visits, or just eating dinner with us. I think "iApple" is toxic to a fragile, forming spirit.

Tough choices, tested moments, pressure from friends, and development shaped by surging testosterone and relentless social media—all of these were colliding at once for my son. Meanwhile, in my motherhood space, I drifted, seeking answers to the universe.

'Til Death, Do I Part?

I believe we're akin to milk cartons—we have stamped expiration dates on us that we just can't see. On a specific day each year we obliviously pass through the anniversary date of our future death. On these pages, I've gone on and on and strongly asserted that midlife truly is a period of grief. We mourn identity loss. But hey, I should just say it. It's death. A once-known Self has died. Or is dying. A long, drawn-out death over years.

To be truthful, I've not gone too deeply into reflecting upon my physical death. The thought gives me the *willies*. Am I afraid? Am I bummed I'll miss out on life? Do I even want to imagine what this world would will be like in 100 years? Even 50? Does finality hurt?

There's no odder topic. This ridiculously small mind can't imagine the vastness, so I fill it with all sorts of circular abstractions and hyperbole to appease gaping blanks. A small mind always wants to *know*. About everything. Even things that can't be known, including God, the afterlife, and where single dryer socks go.

However, there are those who've nearly died and through their escape hatch, come back to spread the *knowing* gospel of tunnels, bright lights, loved ones, angels, and a sense of eternal peace. "It's beautiful," they say. "I felt so free…" Sometimes I want to believe them.

I'd be remiss if I explored midlife identity death and failed to address *the* death. Because midlife is also the juncture when probability becomes inevitability. Shit gets less avoidable. As I surveyed spiritual, emotional, and intellectual deaths, the Grim Reaper felt left out and in a stroke of his own immortal ego (of course he's a man), decided to *deathsplain* and remind me that my life was beyond half over.

One day as I studied wrinkles in the mirror, his presence grew stronger. A chill frosted behind my left shoulder. I felt death lean in closer toward my ear. I anticipated the message Grimmy was about to convey. I held my breath and remained still to listen. I was curious what sage prophecy he'd finally extol after years of avoidance. In a moment of silence, he stole the small breath I'd been holding and with it faintly whispered . . .

Never gonna give you up, never gonna let you down...

Apparently the Grim Reaper lives up to having a dark sense of humor and is a Rick Astley fan.

Perhaps a more consequential question isn't necessarily when, but how? Sometimes my mind saunters toward dark corners not because I'm suicidal, but because "cause of death" is just macabre.

I could be driving on a road and imagine wheels veering over the yellow line, drifting into an oncoming car. I picture crumpled metal, exploding glass, and violent impact of death. I'll be wandering the mall on a casual Sunday, or taking a shower at the gym in the morning, and suddenly, in the midst of an otherwise peaceful moment, an intrusive movie reel flashes in my mind—a madman stalking through the food court or locker room with an automatic rifle spraying bullets. I imagine the terror of being unable to flee. Just based on sheer probability, I've written off the possibilities of lightening or sharks. Bridges provide interesting mental fodder.

I suppose death is black and parched and vacant like a vessel, and quiet. A silence so quiet it reverberates with a buzz or hum or ringing of a the no-longer-functioning body, trace echoes of halted blood flow, seized cells, and the hollow thump of a drumless heart. Only an aftertaste of death remains: of formaldehyde, stomach acid, dirty root vegetables, and drought-seized soil.

It's either ironic or fitting that as lost as I've felt in my life, I'm equally lost, if not more so, about death. I can't see how I'll end. For as long as I can remember I've had vague certainty that I'd be buried. Eternally at rest next to my beloved. Well, my beloved, Mark, wants to be cremated. Maybe it's my Jewish DNA, but there's no way I want to be slid into an oven like a ready-to-bake pizza. I just can't. Mark says I'll be dead, so what's the difference? Yet, imaginable postcards of an unimaginable trip through an 1800-degree inferno gnaw the recesses of my mind. Somehow, I think I'd still know.

As for burial, that would mean I'd take up forever residence in a cemetery, but I'm not clear yet where I'd be living (assuming I'm a ripe old age) and I feel like no one would come see me. My kids barely visit now, while I'm alive, so I'm certain that after they go off to live their lives, visits ain't gonna happen when I'm decomposing flesh and bone. I'd be there alone in the dark, a skeleton in repose, without a husband, waiting for someone to come. Sounds pathetic, right? I guess that takes burial off the table now, too.

These days there are alternatives: being composted into trees, infused into record albums, placed in jewelry, stuck in freezers, sunk deep into the ocean as part of an artificial reef used for fish habitats, and even blown into space aboard a rocket, (either mummified or plasticized, your choice).

I struggle to land on the identity of who I am in death—resting girl, inferno girl, necklace girl, record girl, tree girl, fish girl, freezer girl, space girl, mummy girl, or plastic girl? How much do these options cost? Who's going to pay for it? What if this leads to fights among the kids? Do I get insurance now for all this crap, as if I'm not worth enough for them to figure out how to pay for my end? (So I *still* think of my kids, even in death?)

The whole eternal demise thing becomes complicated.

Perhaps the most elusive, is after that future death date, how did people memorialize me?

What words at my funeral were tearfully recited to honor me?

What unique essence of me did friends feel compelled to share?

What corner of my heart did my children carry forward into who they became, that I never got to see, and resided in the love I sacrificed to ensure?

Did I die happy?

During my Dark Flight, I still played the death game as if it could divulge some insight into my still-alive-but-suffering situation. The grand illusion my head clung to until my heart figured some things out was that the curvy road led somewhere, even though the end of individual existence became a bewildering, exquisite, heartbreaking adventure of having been everywhere and nowhere. Each curve painted an invisible swerving line of time I followed to feel as if there was a definitive direction. The bends were about how to navigate time, plan for time, cheat time, clutch dissolving time, peer into tomorrow time, all within a stardust trail of time—which left faint clues along the way that the road never really ended... Did it ever really begin?

Part II
My Selfie

The concept of the "Selfie" relates to the entire other person we project to the world. More on this in a bit, but for now here's the gist: the Selfie is the version of ourselves we need people to see—including ourselves. The Selfie is the additional barrier—and it's huge!—that pushes us further away from our clearest, truest selves. The Selfie has thinned the line between sharing our lives and projecting our lives. At its base is the bolstering of a brittle ego. Factor in common midlife issues of feeling invisible or irrelevant.

How can we see our Selves based on who we project?

How do we project versions of our Self?

Why do we project them?

We've evolved into a society that perpetuates our need for constant reflection of the projected versions of ourselves. Algorithms display products in our cyber feeds (based on our past purchases) that reinforce our individual tastes and preferences. When we read posts of people's opinions, we automatically assess whether they conflict or align with our own. Hundreds of products can be customized with our images; emails generate auto messages with our names bot-inserted. Small wonder Apple's named everything with "I" in front of it.

All this need for being reinforced—yet the reinforcement is of Selfie versions of who we are. We're living in a time of ultimate paradox: it is the Information Age, yet we know less about less than ever before. It's the Connection Era, yet human connection has eroded—we're less connected to ourselves and to each other. Loneliness is social capital.

Middle-age identity loss may have looked completely different 20 years ago. Without the external pressures constantly being placed on our Selves, who knows how we'd navigate the shift in who we become in midlife.

Even knowing every valid criticism of social media, I still have an unhealthy addiction to my phone—checking in, scrolling, mindless perusing. I feel anxious when my phone's not near me. Clinging my phone is like having a not-even-that-great-looking idiot boyfriend who is entirely hollow, whose conversation is as nourishing as Twinkies. Every time you're with him, you think, *What the hell am I doing with this creme-filled plastic sponge of a human?* But the minute you're alone, get bored, or don't want to hear the echo of your own thoughts, you call him and ask him to come over to skirt fear of aloneness and satiate the familiar addiction comfort.

What's the point of posting anything? Does anyone really care? Saying you're depressed makes people uncomfortable. We've become accustomed to life as surface-showcased through vague status updates, pictures of pasta and pies, rehearsed pouty-lipped, chin-angled selfies. The ability to express a full life of wounds is out of social media bounds. The Selfie portrayal during my Dark Flight complicated every aspect of my inner reflection and healing. I worried about what people saw, thought, or heard about the implosion of my business sale, where it had left me, and the messy aspects of my Flight.

I had no desire to share the depth of my sadness because I had a professional persona. I didn't want pity. Plus, I felt like a broken record. Each day was the same kind of empty. Externally, expectations cast unspoken glares about how long I was allowed to be sad, lost, or lonely; Internally, I felt because I had a so-called good life—my health, a great husband, beautiful children—I had no right to feel lost or afraid.

Only people with "real" problems were entitled to grieve.

What to Expect
About Expecting

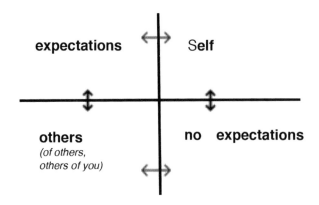

A substantial discovery I made along my Flight was the power expectations have on identity. One day I created an ad hoc model to visually articulate the way expectations run the show of who I am. If you follow around the arrows in the above model, from one quadrant to the next there are variations: expectations of our selves, expectations we have of others, expectations others have of us, no expectations of others, no expectations of our selves.

"Expectation" is a word with massive weight. But what does it mean?

If I had to make an interpretation:

Expectation: Hope + Foreseen Assumption = Outcome

We have a hope for something and a specific projected belief that combines to create a resulting vision.

Do expectations start out as seeds of hope, but then our fixation on a specific belief about the outcome takes away the purity of hope and instead morphs the striving process into disappointments or measures of worth?

Expectations prompt us to dream. To excel. To raise the bar on ourselves and what we create. Expectation comes with a cousin, "worth" or "worthiness", because if we *expect* more, it's because we believe—that a person, situation, outcome, or ourselves—are worth it.

Let's say I'm having a bad day and I call a friend, hoping for a kind ear. If I start talking about what's going on, based on prior experiences, I expect to get compassion from that friend. How much of expectation is based on prior experience? Circumstances change, so shouldn't expectations change, too? What if she's not home? Or maybe she's having her own bad day and I end the phone call feeling worse?

The above model's key takeaway helped me see how expectations propagated my Dark Flight of the Self. I'd had decades and decades of expectations of myself. I was much more weighted in those of myself than in those I had of others.

Most women I know have inflated expectations of themselves. We crack constant mental whips to do more, be more, exceed more in how we look, what we weigh, what we wear, how we achieve, how we mother, how we multitask, how we perform, how we maintain, how we sacrifice, how we adapt, how we give in, how we hide, how we pretend, and ultimately, how tightly we hold on to prevent ourselves from losing our grip.

Over the course of my professional life some expectations were helpful, although only a few were realistic. Interestingly, when every aspect of my life suddenly changed and my structures also changed (who I was in the world and how I moved about each day), the expectations I'd placed on myself hadn't.

This was completely unrealistic: to expect I'd perform at such a high-functioning level even though everything around me stopped. As a result, I became unkind to myself. Every thought, every inaction, every self-criticism, every bout of self-directed anger became related to *not* delivering outcomes. I was still trying to create outcomes that were no longer relevant, appropriate, or even possible.

I don't blame having old expectations in a new reality as the cause for *why* I was in a Dark Flight of the Self, but it absolutely added to *how*

I experienced being in a Dark Flight for so long. I'd had many decades of putting self-imposed outcomes way ahead of me, and on autopilot, I'd chase a result-driven future.

Good for me for mostly rising to the occasion. It yielded security to financially provide for my family, it earned me a professional reputation, it produced opportunities to travel, it generated incredible experiences and creativity, and, most important, it afforded me freedom to remain self-employed.

How is it that the blessing which had given so much could become the curse that brought me down the hardest? I've spent my whole life expecting. Not in the *What To Expect When You're Expecting* sort of way. Instead of a book about pregnancy, that would be a better title about life's disappointments. Because think about it: on the other side of expectation is disappointment. Resentment. Guilt.

Along with expectation comes the backdrop of something more, or different, or not yet realized. There's a lot of running and constantly getting from one place/space/time to another.

Expectations make the transitions during an in-between exhausting.

Imagine a demanding coach yelling at you for five extra laps after you've already run 30 and it's 90 degrees outside. Keep going. Keep moving. Keep doing. At some point, you're going to drop. It will be physically impossible to keep going. The moment of stopping automatically, no matter what, feels like failure. It's less than the envisioned outcome.

Expectations are self-created trolls looming beneath the bridges of our being. *Run. Run. Run. Do. Do. Do. Keep. Going. Keep. Doing. Don't. Ever. Stop.*

People talk about having high expectations. Does this mean envisioning something beyond what reason dictates? Or is this merely a way to stretch one's dreams and truly give in to the fullness of one's hopes?

We expect thousands of things in life. Some expect to live long enough to stare at their own wrinkled hands. We have expectations of our children—who they will become or how they should construct their lives. We expect the mail to show up on all days but Sunday. We expect the sun to rise. We expect an ice cream truck to stop if we run fast enough to flag it down. We expect a good movie if Meryl Streep stars in it. We expect Tylenol to make a headache go away. Once I lower a needle onto a spinning record I expect a familiar crackle only vinyl records bring. I expect to smell warm earth if it rains on a summer afternoon.

I believe the expectations I had of my Self both screwed me over and created success.

It's impossible to adhere to every expectation. People will inevitably disappoint me and I will inevitably disappoint them. Knowing that makes room for forgiveness. Why couldn't I have applied that same fundamental grace to my Self after the midlife shit hit the fan?

* * * * *

The Northern Lights:
So Not as Advertised

Although I have several stories to illustrate the good, bad, and ugly of expectations, one is a real crowd pleaser. It's a sad-funny story about chasing the northern lights.

From the time I was young I'd felt a kinship with the northern lights. Why a girl raised in smoggy Los Angeles with millions of people and car-clogged streets would feel connected to the skies of Alaska is a mystery.

I'd always seen pictures: the iconic scene of a white, snowy landscape, a rustic cabin in the distance with a yellow light shining from a single window, and high above, a gigantic ribbon of neon green twirling across the sky leading down to the chimney top.

The ethereal swirls were burned into my mind. No matter how old I got, the innocence of the dream stayed with me. The allure of the aurora's miraculous act of nature represented God's expression.

Seeing the northern lights became number one on my bucket list.

A year after Mark and I started going out, I told him I wanted to see them. I did some research and came to discover that short of going to Iceland, Fairbanks, Alaska, was one of the best places in the world for viewing.

Without going into too much detail about how and where the aurora can be seen, viewing depends upon the convergence of many factors of time and space. Back then, I was oblivious to the science of what made them occur. (To discover facts and perhaps prevent future disappointment if you've thought about seeing the northern lights, or if you want to learn specifics about how and when northern lights occur, visit my website memyselfieandeye.com).

The only facts I had then were that you can see them nearly two-thirds of the nights in the winter, so if you stay for a week, viewing is probable at least a night or two. My lack of knowledge grossly skewed expectations.

I scheduled our trip for the last week of October, before Fairbanks got too cold to breathe. I made reservations for five nights. We stayed at a place called Chena Hot Springs—supposedly *the* place to see them.

For days leading up to the adventure, excitement filled me. I was convinced that my dream of being beneath the aurora was at last going to come true! I expected billowing green ribbons.

Flying from Portland to Seattle, then to Fairbanks, we arrived around 4 p.m. It gets dark around that time in October. Chena Hot Springs is a funky lodge about an hour's drive north of the city. Mountains are everywhere. The "resort" is rustic, in that it utilizes geothermal electricity for power, generated from naturally occurring hot springs.

Though the hotel and lodging rooms are dated, the hot springs are the star of the show. Huge pools of steaming mineral water bubbled up from the earth. The water is inviting, hot, and rumored to have healing attributes. The main attraction for me, however, was the small aurora-viewing cabin perched on a hill behind the resort.

The darker it got, the more my anticipation grew. I'd been told by a man at the front desk that aurora got active around midnight. Mark and I sat nervously in our hotel room trying to stay awake by watching one of the three crappy television channels our mountain location allowed. Around 11 p.m., a bank of clouds covered the sky. Fairbanks is nestled within a valley, so moving clouds and storms are common. I didn't know or factor this in. I was tired from the day's travels and disappointed when I peeked through the curtain and the clouds only seemed to get bigger. Around midnight, we bundled in layers and made our way through the darkness, crunching snow under our boots, to the tiny viewing cabin.

The only thing inside the "cabin" was a single folding chair. Kind of anticlimactic. I'm not sure what I expected, but it was more than that.

Mark suggested we take turns keeping watch. He let me have the chair and lay down on the dusty wooden floor. He told me to wake him after 30 minutes of shut-eye. Looking around the makeshift cabin, sitting on a folding chair, bundled up like a Ukrainian dog musher, and barely able to move beneath the stifling fabric, I started to perspire.

I had the sinking feeling no aurora were going to be seen.

After 25 anxious minutes of sitting like a toasted marshmallow in the dark, listening to Mark snore, thinking about axe murderers and/or bears that were going to rip open the door any minute, staring out into space and not seeing a single cloud move, I felt stupid and resentful. I didn't want to seem like a baby, after all, it was only our first night. Yet already, my expectations of a grand show of spinning light ribbons and communion with God had withered.

I kicked Mark's foot with my foot to wake him. He sat up, looked around, and said, "Has it been 30 minutes? It seems like I shut my eyes a second ago." I didn't want to admit that my fear of imminent murder or mauling had cut off his snooze by five minutes. "Um, yeah," I said. He asked, "Anything changed?" Annoyed, I mumbled, "Nope."

"Well, why don't you see if you can take a nap and I'll keep watch." What I wanted to answer was, "This night is stupid, this no-electricity cabin sucks, I wish I'd never watched *Friday the 13th*, what the fuck is up with the clouds, it's so dusty in here, are they so goddamn cheap that they could only spring for *one* folding chair instead of two? I just want to go to bed." But I was sure I'd sound like an ungrateful *Green Acres* Eva Gabor diva-in-the-woods, so instead I awkwardly maneuvered through 17 layers of wool and sweaters and gloves to plop down onto the dirty planks.

The more I lay there thinking about spiders (do spiders even live in the cold of Fairbanks?) and how expressions of God were letting me down, the more I seethed. I lasted about five minutes, then proclaimed, "Let's go. I don't wanna sit here feeling like a dumbass."

I'm not sure if Mark was annoyed at me for being such a woods-sissy, or relieved because he was tired, too, but he replied, "Okay."

Back to the hotel room we traipsed, shuffling and crunching in the snow, although in my imagined avoidance of an axe tip or bear claw, I walked a bit faster than on the way up. Of course, the faster pace was making me really sweat, so I had a frozen nose and sweaty armpits.

In the room, it took me 10 minutes to rip off the hat, unzip the puffy space coat, lift off the wool pullover, peel off the thermal layer, undo the ski boots, take off the two layers of socks, remove the sweatpants, then unroll the sweaty leggings. The mountain of clothing on the floor mocked the failed night. Only 10 hours into our trip, and already it had been a bust.

The rest of our nights were more of the same. Anxiety about what would transpire at night ruled our days. The anticipation—no, the *expectation*—pretty much ruined any of the other activities or sights or things we did on that trip because everything—including my happiness—hinged on the appearance of an incredible act of nature over which I had *zero* control. I hated whatever sightseeing we did during the day, then would sit up at night staring at the cloud-shrouded sky and seethe. I was miserable and desperate and unreasonable the entire trip.

That first foray to Fairbanks, we came up short. The nights there were lights, there were clouds. The nights there were no clouds, there were no lights. I went home utterly disappointed.

It was after this trip that I started to wonder about the place expectations had in a person's life. I believed that people fell into two camps: those who always had expectations and those who never had any. As someone who had always them, I thought people who said never to expect anything were sad, as if they must have suffered a lot of disappointment. I also couldn't figure out how people like that were able to turn off their expectations like a light switch. How could you tell yourself or train yourself to do that?

But the northern lights were a supreme disappointment. I'd imagined a relief for finding answers to God, an ultimate feeling of *knowing*. I expected to discover resolution within my heart—a place that was hungry and weary and in need of assurance. I left Fairbanks deflated.

Was it better to expect nothing? Would that mean you'd get nothing? Do people who expect nothing actually spare themselves from disappointment or is that just what they tell themselves? Is expectation really hope? How can we go through life without hope?

Mark and I went back to Fairbanks the following October for a do-over. By then I'd learned more about how the northern lights appear and the science behind them. I knew what solar events to monitor, and how to loosely predict appearance based on several indicators. I suppose having background knowledge put a morsel of expectation in its place, but I still had hopes.

To up the odds, I booked an expensive excursion with Aurora Chasers. They are northern lights guides. They've been doing this for years, know how to avoid areas that have clouds moving in and utilize a bunch of technological equipment that can more accurately predict aurora appearance.

The night we went out with them, we did see the aurora borealis, but with everything leading up to that moment, they weren't as expected. I'd finally accomplished a lifelong bucket list dream, yet I felt disappointment.

It turns out that what the eyes see is different than what a camera captures. Photos show the aurora light as bright, neon, luminescent. In real life, the lights resemble more of a green fog. They're duller, cloudier, and the strips and swirls move fast (which surprised me!). Don't get me wrong—the northern lights are beautiful, an incredible sight to behold and a totally cool phenomenon to witness. I'm extremely grateful to have seen them. But what you see in real life and what's shown in pictures will always differ.

As I stood beneath the sky, looking up with hope and anticipation, what was experienced in real time—the colors, the sensations, how they move—did not mirror the imagery in my mind—the lifelong expectation that had been created.

Maybe expectations are merely advertisements—idealized notions of what something *should* be. Anticipating, then actually seeing, the northern lights became a key metaphor about expectations in life, versus being in actual life.

Do These Duck Lips Make My Ass Look Fat?

After discovering how expectations contributed to the duration of my Dark Flight, I contemplated what was making my search for lost identity more challenging. As if wandering through an internal journey wasn't strange enough, I saw another culprit, a whole other hostile universe that made navigating toward a true Self more impossible: social media and the projected self otherwise referred to as the *selfie*.

Have you ever wondered where the term and modern social concept of the selfie came from? I have. Imagine life before the whole ubiquitous, instantaneous "look at me" mess. (At least in Renaissance times, an artist spent months creating a self-portrait!)

It should come as no surprise that sources trace the intentional taking of a picture of one's self—and then donning it what a cutesy name— to a drunk guy at a birthday party in Australia. In an inebriated stupor, he tripped and fell, had medical attention, then sought advice on whether or not licking his lips would dissolve the stitches there. He snapped a close-up to show the doctor's handiwork.

"Anyone wanna see a picture of it? It's pretty cool," he wrote, and posted a link to an image he uploaded onto a university server. Beneath the photo he wrote, "I had a hole about 1 cm long right through my bottom lip. And sorry about the focus, it was a selfie." (Australian dialect often shortens words and ends them with "ie," such as "barbie" for barbecue.)

So: the origins of an entire lexicon, an entire form of human expression, an entire alteration of how we relate to and present our selves to the world—derived from drunken party shenanigans.

How can we be with, discover, or reveal a true Self when we're busy projecting an entirely different one? Not only do we have to keep up with the Joneses, but also the likes, hearts, wows, comments, and relentless pressure of managing an existence of an entire other Self. We're image-projection handlers running interference over what we do or don't present to the public court of social juries.

Then there's deciphering the unspoken social media mores. Keeping up on social media protocol across Instagram, Pinterest, Snapchat, Twitter, Facebook, and LinkedIn is spiritually depleting. Wondering why you don't get enough immediate external validation is soul sucking; making sure to follow someone who's followed you, even though you don't really want to, because if you didn't that would be rude. Unfollowing someone you can't stand, but not going the distance to unfriend them. But why bother keeping them around cyber socially if you can't stand them enough to call it quits? The undercurrent of balancing unspoken taboos is constant. The social media scorecard adds stress. Plus: waaayyyy too many pouty duck lips . . .

While going through my Dark Flight, I didn't care to parade my predicament. I'd spent years building a reputation. I was known for being an ambitious, confident professional. One hundred forty characters was not remotely enough to explain that I was losing my mind, I had a few drinks every night, I'd gotten fat, I was a terrible mother because my son was on Xbox for hours at a time, I hadn't made a home-cooked meal in months, I was the sexless failure of a wife I swore I'd never become, that brushing my teeth had become a chore, and that I was afraid I'd become lost forever. I'm not sure there's a hashtag for that.

I am, however, lucky to have context for a life without the internet or social media. My childhood was an existence free from instant gratification, trolling, and selfies. We in middle age *know*. Electronic drug fixes came in the form of Scooby Doo and H.R. Pufnstuf during Saturday morning cartoon marathons propped in front of a Zenith console television (foil-balled antenna optional), chomping on bowls of Count Chocula.

My children will never know such simple wonder. All they know are lives *with* the internet. They were born and raised in a social media fishbowl. I have friends who post constant videos and photos of their kids. The term for this is *sharenting*. These kids have been on public display since birth. They're used to surveillance and constant documentation of how they move in the world. I get that we are proud of our children and want to share. I understand that sharing milestones with relatives and friends means something, and thanks to the advent of technology, we can. Far be it from me to be the posting police.

However, there's a line between enough and too much. There are potential detriments to a child's tender evolution of an identity. Parents have become detached from being present with children and have replaced face-to-face interaction with face-to-screen automation. We're cultivating a generation of screen characters who have little opportunity to absorb, reflect, or be part of a moment, let alone be able to connect with who they are in those moments.

Growing up before the proliferation of social media gave me a chance to formulate more of a Me and less of a Selfie. To be a kid or young adult now with such constant superficial scrutiny would suck. When I was 15, 16, and 17, my mistakes didn't get recorded, then paraded on a wide-open platform for the world to see and judge. Who I kissed, what I wore, and when I threw up from too much Mickey's Big Mouth were my moments and mine alone, to be remembered as memories should: through time's tender, hazy, tempered glass.

I correlate today's epidemic of depression and anxiety among teens to the magnification and projection of the Selfie. Research has shown that more screen interaction equates to less meaningful human interaction. Social media promotes unrealistic snapshots and falsely constructed images of how people live.

The basis of the Selfie is perpetual self-absorption. There's distance from authentic *being* and spiritual depletion over what's promoted as important in life. The muscle for internalizing has atrophied. We no longer contemplate, debate, or engage with deeper ideas. We have scarce reflective processes to make sense or meaning of something before we lapse into judgment.

Scroll. Swipe. Tap. Tune out.

Repeat.

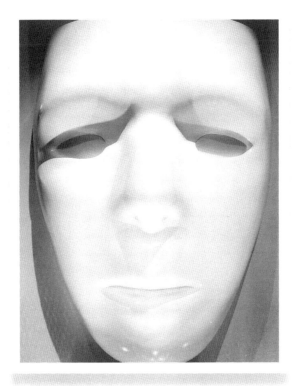

Fuck the Cloud

I've been dubbed a technophobe. Which is fine; I could be called worse things and I don't believe the moniker's entirely accurate in my case, because I'm not really *afraid* of technology. But there is a fundamental dislike—no, that's being too soft—fundamental *disdain*—I carry, based on principle, that accounts for my technology aversion.

I don't like, nor do I think it's fair, that we're socially, culturally, economically, or politically forced to do, be, or react to life according to technology. Everything is digital and online. Human interaction is going away. Technology has killed the reverence for ritual.

Within the last 20 years, what we know about humanity has changed because of technology.

On one side, yes, are advances in science, medicine, and access to information, which have made marvelous contributions to human life. We can witness cosmos in deep space never before seen. A surgeon can repair a human heart. Music of any style, from Nashville or Nairobi, can be played anywhere—on a bus, in a schoolyard, at the gym, at a party, on a walk—with a single screen touch.

Yet social technological advances come at a high price regarding our individual relationships to Self and to others. Life behind screens, looking down, and not out into the world, in the name of passive gratification creates a dispassionate filter of reality. The will to exert intellectual or imaginative effort is going away. We're less resourceful and less resilient. Human engagement, discovery, exploration, reflective thought, and contemplation are relics because technology makes everything too immediate, too easy.

When I go to visit a doctor, the physician spends 90 percent of the time looking at a screen instead of me. In a checkout line at a grocery store, there's no need for clerks to look up or connect with customers through the eyes—they're shuffling items over scanners. Every phone call to every business is met with a voicemail tree from hell that sends me into an abyss of pressing or saying "1" or "2." These may seem like insignificant things on their own, but combined, every day, we're becoming dehumanized.

I'm uncomfortable with the idea that somewhere, somehow, permeating particles of air and space, are billions of data bits swarming around, polluting some mystery "cloud." I find it disconcerting that molecular cyber-bits of my memories, my photos, my work, my words, my videos, my music, and anything else related to a library of my life are "stored" (up above?) with trillions of other bits of god knows what belonging to god knows who. The whole cloud thing is creepy.

I like storing old letters in a worn shoebox to rifle through on a rainy day; perusing a photo album fat with crinkly plastic sleeves, thumbing through a stand of vinyl records to discover the music's mood; plucking out sheets of poetry I wrote lifetimes ago from a metal cabinet drawer. There's something about tangibly recognizing, honoring, and protecting expressive elements that make up our identities, through the actions of storing, retrieving, and perusing those moments. The cloud is eroding life's rite-of-passage rituals.

My frustration over the world that is and the world that was only became clearer when I ventured into an Apple store to address my phone's battery problems. When I stepped up to the Genius Bar, a 20-something know-it-all named Jagger (who probably created the Spotify Arcade Fire playlist) deeply sighed, as if he'd rather be home stirring yeast in his basement brew or knitting a beanie. His scraggly beard was red. I started to explain being unable to sync photos to my laptop and before I finished my sentence, he looked at me in horror as if I'd just stolen his longboard. Through round, quarter-sized glasses he sneered, "Well, don't you store your data on the cloud???"

The hipster-douche cloud-shamed me.

After enduring Jagger's condemnation, I did what any other self-respecting 50-something would do. I went across the mall to the AT&T store to upgrade my phone and for $27 more a month, for 46 months, I traded my pride and sold my soul for another two-year contract.

Don't even get me started on how creepy, wrong, and weird Siri and Alexa are.

* * * * *

These influences related to Self—including technology and social media, including the outside world and our place in it—have become convoluted, immediate, and contrived. There's no curation process that allows who we are to settle in while experiencing life. Throw in our internal need to feed the insatiable beast of expectation and good luck unearthing one's Self while in the throes of midlife identity loss.

Part III

Eye

Inertia

How I came to unearth my Self while in the throes of my midlife identity loss was through my "Eye." How do we trudge through confusion and external pressures? How do we "see" our Selves again? Everyone's Eye is different because everyone's circumstances—where they are, who they are, what they feel—are different. Perhaps only some of my specific Eye experience resonates with you.

Midlife delivers a unique Eye. Why we search and what's open for discovery come at a specific midlife intersection brought about by very specific identity dismantling conditions. We have to do things we've never done. We have to stretch in new ways that don't feel good. We wonder if all we've known before is true or what of it mattered. And all these aspects exist within a flimsy, unfamiliar framework without identifiable words to describe the accompanying shifts.

These are the conditions of the Eye.

＊ ＊ ＊ ＊ ＊

Words that hinted at how I felt during my Dark Flight of the Self:
　frozen
　comatose
　in hibernation
　exiled

Since describing my emotional state was difficult, I looked up synonyms to the above words. One word jumped out.

Inert:

1. lacking the ability or strength to move.

2. lacking vigor.

3. chemically inactive.

synonyms:

unmoving, motionless, immobile, inanimate, still, stationary, static; dormant, sleeping; unconscious, lifeless, insensible, insensate, insentient; idle, inactive, underactive, sluggish, lethargic, indolent, stagnant, listless, torpid

Yes. That was it! I was *inert*. Every definition and synonym was me.

It's a Small World,
After All

One day I woke up trapped in a blizzard wearing a white, paper-thin jump-suit. Sheets of sideways blowing ice obliterated visibility. Without a trace of direction, unable to distinguish the outline of my own body from swirling chaos, I stumbled around. I extended my limbs toward the sea of snow, praying for luck to spur eventual contact with something palpable—anything that tethered my form to another. Nothing appeared.

This is how I describe my Dark Flight emotional disorientation. Mentally reaching for anything I understood as true, with no clue as to what thoughts or feelings were connected or real.

I wonder why it becomes impossible during these periods to declare context for our Selves? Context here means emotions, thoughts, truths, realities that compose a sum of who we are—particularly in relation to Other. In this case, Other is the rest of an entire world. Other is the totality of our lives and all the people, circumstances, and possessions that are part of it.

A big aspect of how we see ourselves is in relation to Other. If all that's known or believed about who we are suddenly explodes, it's a losing prospect to connect fragments of debris with anything else that comprises our lives. There isn't enough substance left to compare them with or align them against. Identity becomes as elusive as clouds, and all the people and environments and change of circumstance become the rocks. You can't tie rocks to clouds.

An identity IS the life context.

This idea led to reflecting over the past few years about identity and Self as context and how these truths we know about who we are coexist and derive from our relationship to Other.

Here's a somewhat related story, to explain.

When I was on Maui a few years ago, I took a trek to Hana. A five-minute conversation with a stranger during the excursion was so profound it'll be with me the rest of my life.

I stayed at the beautiful Hotel Hana-Maui. On the wet side of Maui, nestled on the island's eastern corner at the base of Haleakala volcano, is Hana, a beach town at the edge of a lush forest. It's secluded and tiny and that historic hotel is the only real tourist-driven game in town.

Hana is one of the most isolated communities in all of the Hawaiian Islands, with a population of 1,200 people. It's accessible primarily via the famous Hana Highway, a twisty, turny, 52-mile-long, narrow highway along Maui's rugged northern shore.

I spent four days in Hana absorbing the tranquility. One late morning I took a short walk from the hotel toward the ocean. At the edge of a turquoise bay sat a beefy Hawaiian fella dangling a homemade fishing rod into the water. A sack lunch rested beside him on a sun-weathered table. I strolled in his direction, approached the bench he was sitting on, and said hello. I asked him how his day was. He smiled and replied, "When you got nothin' but waitin' to catch *ono*, every day is a good day."

His name was Hana Bob. Well, I contrived the *Hana* part. He shared that he was born and raised in Hana. In his 37 years of life, he'd never left Maui. He'd barely left Hana, he said, and went to other parts of Maui only when medical or food supplies required it.

I gazed at the blue water. The light shimmered above the wind-kissed sea like glitter. A warm breeze of soft sand and hibiscus, and pineapple, and waterfalls, and rainbows, and sea turtles, and hula, and ukulele, and bamboo, and puffer fish and mai tais whisked me into Hana Bob envy. *He's so lucky.*

After a few moments of basking in a seductive fantasy something snagged.

I realized that if Maui is all he's known, Hana Bob's never been part of anything else. *Hmmm.*

He's never ducked beneath the shadow of a towering skyscraper on a humid New York day. Never heard the clanking chimes of slot machines in a smoke-filled Las Vegas casino. Never sat in a nosebleed seat at a concert. Never flagged a cab or chased an ice cream truck. Never witnessed saguaros standing at attention for a painted desert sunrise. Never frozen childhood by hearing, "There is just one moon and one golden sun" while waiting in line to ride It's a Small World at Disneyland. Hana Bob had never been to a major sporting event.

Those were my thoughts when I asked, "Any desire to see a Dodgers or Yankees game?"

"Nah," he replied as if the notion was preposterous.

His laissez-faire response caught me off guard.

I was flooded by conflict. Could Hana Bob—or anyone—ever be *so* content that they never wanted to experience anything outside of themselves in their lives? Could someone be *so* satisfied, with themselves and their experiences, that they never wanted to search? Was he oblivious to how every single thing that is Other, beyond our context, makes us who we are? Take a moment to imagine the implications—both good and bad—of a life whose context was only Hana, Maui.

Perhaps you've never left your hometown. Maybe you've traveled the world. Is it okay to assume that in either case, who you are and your identity is informed as a result? It's crazy to imagine that every molecule we encounter—every sight, aroma, sound, human, situation, memory, conversation—becomes a complicated tapestry woven into Self and Other.

Why did this encounter with Hana Bob jar me? Why am I bringing it up now? The process of sewing back together a lost midlife identity isn't like running a marathon course for a second time, knowing what to expect at mile 7, or 16, or 22. *Ahhh, yes, this is where I take water. This is where the hill gets steep. This is where I'll hit a wall and not want to go on. This mile is where I really need to push myself.*

It's incremental, and there were many days when it seemed as if I'd never feel connected or familiar to my Self or Other again. I felt forever exiled from what I thought I knew. I contemplate whether it's a luxury or a curse to have a less-complicated existence. If Hana Bob's context is small, familiar, and reliable, does that mean his identity is, too? Would he have fewer pieces of himself to lose and glue back together if something blew up in his life?

I've come across many people who dream of simplifying existence. Maybe this equates to less financial burden; or fewer business obligations; a calendar with fewer places to be; or less materialistic stuff overcrowding space. "Simplification" may imply a surface ideal or be loosely constructed to represent a pathway toward perceived freedom.

What might reside at the heart of striving for simplicity is a desire to feel closer alignment with identity. Think about it. If you want to simplify your life, what is that about? From what to what? And why?

My "all" became very small when I was suddenly left to traverse a borderless blizzard wearing undiscernible white.

All I wanted was to find my way home.

* * * * *

For many people, a Dark Flight of Self, of identity, entails an ever-present, permeating relationship with (what they believe to be) God. There's a *knowing*, a connection, a secured faith in that relationship that helps fill in the holes of doubt. I admire those who can rely on their hearts and forego intrusive, mostly unhelpful thoughts. Especially thoughts which lead to questions that just don't have concrete answers.

A faith in God, in something that doesn't need to be explained or proven or researched or quantified, is a mythical unicorn to me. Not that God is a mythical unicorn—it's the capacity to have this faith that is such an unknown. And to be okay with not knowing, just as it is. Even talking about this kind of non-thought certainty is agitating to me.

Trust and faith are not the same thing, but I believe they're intertwined. To me, having trust means following the crumbs, because they have some concrete tangibility. Crumbs could be circumstances or past experiences that afford some measure of comfort.

Faith, on the other hand, alludes to the "whispers" I mentioned earlier. These are the fragments of our intuition, the unexplainable reasons for wanting to pursue certain directions in our lives, the parts of our spirit or soul that beckon us toward life's allowance. These whispers could be from God, the universe, our souls, our hearts, the collective consciousness, or even the mysterious hummingbird who appeared at a deep moment of doubt to assure me things would be okay.

Which is why I previously brought up following the whispers and crumbs during the Dark Flight of the Self as an aspect of the Eye—the *how* we come to see ourselves—because in midlife, these two go hand in hand. Our faith *and* our trust. We need external assurances and internal guidance to conspire throughout the Dark Flight. These form the signposts that signal our Dark Flight is headed somewhere. No matter how lost we feel or how far away we are from a Self we once knew, we *will see* ourselves again soon.

I wish I had an unencumbered relationship with God. I wish my heart was more in the mix of who I am and how I relate to the world. I wish my thoughts didn't shit on all the mystery and magic that comes my way. I wish I could fully know and embrace a nonjudgmental love for my Self not driven by expectations. I wish I could accept my limitations and mistakes as a human being just trying to make sense of an overwhelming, sometimes scary world. I wish I could have had a deep well of forgiveness from which to draw a bucket or two when I was not kind to myself. I wish I could internally sit with stillness long enough to dwell in the echo of my heartbeat.

Presence is God. Forgiveness is God. Acceptance is God. Mystery is God. Synchronicity is God. All of these become packaged in a way that's easily understood and expressed. No need to explain, it just is.

I still grapple with what I believe about God. There's no singular certainty. And not having this in my life as a clear answer meant that my Flight time took a little longer than perhaps someone who's solid in this part of their identity's navigation.

To Pill or Not to Pill, That Was a Question

While in darkness, I thought about depression medication. I'd contemplated it as a vague concept and when density had a grip, the *Do I or Don't I?* inner debaters screamed. The verdict was that medication wasn't for me. Not because I was tough or could pull myself up by the bootstraps, or because I was better than, or because it symbolized mental illness. I totally respect an individual's decision around what they do or don't choose to survive.

If I had believed medication might help, I would have entertained using it. Although I felt depressed, buried beneath my emotional sludge was a hint that what I was going through was different from depression, though the experience included it.

With earning a living imminent but not yet urgent, I had no motivation to find motivation. I had a slim monetary cushion but the truth was I didn't care if I maxed out credit cards to survive. I can't imagine going through an identity meltdown and having to show up in the world each day at a 9-to-5 job—dressed in clothes other than pajamas. Showing up in daily life and putting on a false face takes tremendous will. I have a lot of respect and empathy for everyone who does.

I've been self-employed for a long time; I'm used to having money or not having money as a direct result of my motivation. That is part of my own story's complication. I *was* what I *did*. My financial and identity survival were dependent on how effectively I produced.

Since I had no clue as to who I was anymore, I also had no clue what was next. Each aimless day was as the one before. Again and again and again I woke up in the same red flannel pajamas I'd gone to sleep in and wore the day before. I went weeks without a bra and showered maybe twice a week. Maybe.

Stacked on top of the depletion loop (I have no energy/I need energy to get energy/but I have no energy) was guilt. Guilt that feeling bad and being aimless meant I was failing my husband and children. I was angry at myself for being unable to get my shit together and confused over how or when or why the being I was being couldn't change.

When I feel like shit I can say, "I feel like shit." When I'm sad I can say, "I'm sad." Depression for me was an identifiable state of being that could be named, but I had no name for what I felt.

So a medication solution didn't seem right. I told myself that if I did everything I could to make myself feel better and I still didn't feel better, I'd consider medication.

I needed to take actions meant for someone who's depleted to feel fortified: get some physical activity, take vitamins, drink water, consume less alcohol, smoke less weed, eat food other than buttered sourdough toast and french fries.

If I had done any one of those things, made a single effort toward fortifying my Self, maybe it would have helped. But I did none.

Goodwill (Clothes) Hunting

Nothing magnifies identity meltdown like a trip to Goodwill. The whole sordid endeavor was prompted by the weight I'd gained the past few years. I couldn't fit into any of my clothes. I had three items to rotate: a prairie skirt, loose sweat pants, and a maxi dress ideal for summer. Fall had arrived and I was forced to acknowledge I needed bigger clothes.

I dreaded looking in my closet. It seemed intent on maximizing my self-loathing. Too-small clothes taunted me that I used to look good; I'd been someone who had choices in what to wear and had my act together enough to fit into cuter clothes.

Walking into Goodwill, I was reminded why I'd gained 40 pounds—I didn't give a shit. Well, that may not be fair. It's probably more accurate to say I *couldn't* give a shit about anything, let alone myself. This is where the Dark Flight of the Self as its own experience has distinction.

In the past if I was down, the Me that I knew, the Me that moved in the world, was able to find a mental tool, an action, a next step that propelled me in a direction away from helplessness. The actions themselves were self-care.

The period of the Dark Flight rendered me unable to take action or talk myself into or out of a state of mind. The paralysis around self-care was a differentiator. The nature of a Dark Flight is what kept me in a Dark Flight.

I know this may sound confusing. But because I was unable to do what I'd done before, because what worked before no longer worked, I was left more depressed, more alone, more confused, and filled with more self-disappointment. I blamed myself for what I perceived as extreme personal failure. Why couldn't I just change my mind? Fake it 'til I made it? Why was I allowing myself to wallow in this cesspool? Was I so fucked up that I secretly wanted to feel sorry for myself? Was this unrecognizable, paralyzed person the real Me?

It makes me incredibly sad when I recall how disconnected from my Self I was. Makes me even sadder when I think about how unforgiving I was of my Self because I was disconnected. I blamed my Self. Every day. The Dark Flight is a total identity dismantling. This disconnection from your Self (*this is what used to be true, these are my ideals*), and to your Self (*talking myself into and out of sadness is what's always worked*) is the central point of the Dark Flight and a necessary part of the identity transition.

Back to the trip to Goodwill. Though I'd been taking small steps forward—going to the gym here and there, slightly motivated for work, feeling a tiny bit better overall—I still had to get with where I was currently and that was in fatter pants. Combing through the XL section, I slid pair after pair along crammed racks. I was looking for pants that weren't stone washed but were wide enough to hold my huge ass. I came across jeans I liked. They were black, with small stitching on the back pockets. They were Angels, which meant a low-rise cut. (I'm not 17. My hips have accommodated two children). They were a size 12. Nope. Keep moving.

At my thinnest, or I'll say healthiest, I was a solid size 8. Thanks to aging combined with intermittent health habits over the years, I've fluctuated between sizes 8 and 14. There were periods when I was motivated, in shape, and floated between 8 and 10. There were periods when I was less motivated and bounced between 12 and 14.

During what I perceive as fat phases, I wore a size 14. (A disclaimer: these sizes and references are from my own experiences. There are women of all sizes and shapes who feel beautiful or inadequate regardless of what the scale or dress size says. My personal perspective by no means implies an opinion about how others should feel regarding their body or weight.)

The XL section had pants in sizes 12, 14, 16, 18, 20, and beyond. I was there because the pants that sat useless in my closet were a size 14 and no longer fit. That whole exercise of sliding hangers along racks of people's unwanted fashion pasts initiated a humiliating yet necessary incentive to do something to change the situation. Feeling like a schlub sucked.

I pulled nine pairs to try on that *appeared* wide enough. I checked the inside label of each pair to verify I was in the ballpark. Pants that looked too big showed a size 12 label while a pair that seemed on the small side revealed a 16.

As I walked toward the dressing room, bracing myself for the shock of how heavy I'd become, I recognized the various pant sizes as symbolic. Size numbers were loose guidelines, ranging wildly within a single size. They were deceiving. There could be 12s that were more like 8s, and 10s that should be 14s. Labeled clothes sizes were vague starting points. The sizes themselves—12, 14, 16—were symbolic. My identity as a size 12 had been as someone within a healthy weight range. A 14, however, represented a woman who was fat. 16? That was a new, out-of-control desperation level I'd never before reached.

There they were, identities of my distant past, recent past, and present represented in my arms, about to enter a dressing room of reckoning.

I became aware that the Dark Flight of the Self was about these identities trying to make sense of one another, trying to make room for one another, trying to reconcile the identities of who I'd been in my past—someone who wore a size 12, my recent past, someone who became a size 14, and the current state, a size 16—all while the labels I so closely identified with were misleading and had vast variations.

That was a strange realization that shined a light on the dismantling process of who I once was. Identities are not pants. *But what I believe about what the pants represent, is. What I think they say about my Self, is.*

I'll Start Monday...

My previous success in reaching goals had been due in part to structure or outside accountability. When I was losing weight in the past, for example, Jenny Craig had counselors to whom I reported progress. Weekly check-ins meant fessing up to transgressions.

Self-employment had made me used to being accountable to myself—at least with work. When I didn't work, I didn't have money. There's a necessity to hustle.

But with writing that wasn't for work, making dietary changes, or imposing a deeper conversation with my Self, there was no external push. Self-reflection was obviously uncomfortable. Why struggle toward changing my thinking, changing my habits, or changing anything familiar, when feeling miserable is just plain easier? Forget the path of least resistance, human nature covets *no* resistance.

Improving my life meant work. Making room for changes meant I would have to give something up, even if that something wasn't good for me. Is resistance rebellion? Sort of like, "Fuck you, you're not the boss of me, you're not going to tell me what to do"? Does it seem like taking on a mental burden is too much, even though our minds are cluttered with useless noise? We have thousands of thoughts a day; of those, how many matter and when do we run out of brain storage?

When I contemplated changing a habit like losing weight, my initial resistance was, "I can't take that on right now . . ." meaning, the mental burden of *thinking* about having to choose a rice cake over cheesecake required more brain exertion than actually just eating the damn rice cake.

Eating cheesecake is pleasurable. Choking down a rice cake is not. I drink tequila. I take a toke every now and again. Sometimes Crunch Berries ensue. What would a world be without french fries? This is where accountability comes in. An outer safeguard of checking in puts a tighter noose around a Wild West of excuses. Not only that, for better or worse,

I'm really good at avoiding a true picture of myself. When I have to say to someone else, "Hey, I didn't do what I said I would," I feel self-judgment's scorn.

This isn't a good thing. How are we to make lasting changes after mustering the courage to be honest with ourselves—then seeing something we don't like? How do we move forward when inquiry makes us feel like shit about ourselves? This arrangement is an emotional set-up.

What's the answer?

I tried to move forward. Or to at least discover the elusive pebble to roll down the hill. To get my ass moving, did I need to be harder on myself? Easier on myself? Did I need to join another (fill in the blank) group? Did I need to create an actual contract that I would make myself sign?

In hindsight, I realized this was foolish. I felt how alone my isolated spirit was. There was no *thinking* my way into or out of that transitory state. I'd distract with soul-sucking Facebook, Twitter, or Instagram. I'd numb the agitation with bullshit cat videos, food porn, or memes of the moment. Mindless scrolling helped me get to emotional invisibility.

But hey, what's a sad, lonely, Dark-Flight-of-the-Self-searching, disconnected, disoriented, self-judging, spiritually destitute, identity-crisis-laden, middle-aged lady gonna do?

* * * * *

I'd seen my counselor Raphael for roughly eight years. When I talked to him about the loss of my identity and the desire to reclaim it, a path toward clarity had come down to making a few definitive steps forward—action to get me in motion. These steps involved three things: exercise, writing, meditation. It made sense. Take care of the body, mind, and spirit.

Knowing that if left to my own devices, I'd falter, Raphael suggested I check in with him each day to monitor progress. Be accountable. Rather than create a strict expectation of how exercise, writing, and mediation might look, we broadened the expectation to make it easier. We came up with "nourish, fulfill, and fortify" as the goals to accomplish each day, and at the end of the day I'd check in.

I offer the following emails I sent to Raphael for a full few weeks, without censorship, to illustrate how rocky and ridiculous the process of self-searching can be.

12/7 — nourish, fulfill, fortify — day 1 — 6:14 pm

I'd give this day a B-.

In terms of nourish, I was set to go to the gym early this morning. But then I couldn't get to sleep. My wake-up call was at 4:15 to go the gym, so because I didn't get the sleep, I didn't get up. On the nourish side, I consciously made myself drink a few glasses of water.

For fortify, it didn't look like I imagined, but qualifies. I've spent weeks getting stuff together for the accountant to get on a structured path as it relates to finances/keeping track/taxes. I had a meeting with the accountant today to hand over paperwork I've spent weeks gathering, so he can give us a tax estimate. Although this isn't what I had in mind as it relates to fortify, getting my financial house in order is important to help with future organization.

As for fulfilling, as of 6:15, I've done nothing. My day was dealing with my son and his iffy school grades, emailing his teachers to come up with a plan moving forward, a computer consultant coming over to fix my computer, some work emails I had to get done. It seems like too many details that have nothing to do with anything other than taking care of shit. I'm not feeling fulfilled at this moment. It's not to say that by the time I go to sleep I won't have found something to check off that box.

What could be small, yet doable, and fulfilling? This is a good question. But I will bet on me that before I put my head on the pillow, I will find something. I'll let you know tomorrow.

12/7 — fulfillment — 7:41pm

I wrapped Christmas gifts. Fulfilling? Maybe a little. I asked myself, "Well then, what fulfills me? What would I do to engage in something fulfilling?" When I imagined fulfillment as a loose concept to adhere to on a daily basis, I pictured reading self-help books or something. An activity I thought qualified as fulfilling. But would reading self-help books actually be fulfilling? It's been so long since I've been fulfilled, spiritually, emotionally. I don't even know what that looks like. Taking hummingbird photos I consider fulfilling. But I can't think of any other activity I do in my life, or imagine myself engaged in as a hobby or activity, that I'd consider fulfilling. :-(What a realization.

12/8— nourish, fulfill, fortify — day 2 — 3:27 pm

So far, I've done nada.

I planned on going on a walk this morning, but got caught on phone calls with Kaiser. Then I started working on a story assignment that had a deadline. Then I got a call from Ethan that he wanted me to take him to the doctor to have his ankle x-rayed. It has not gotten better from last week when he was clowning around and jumped off a stage. So I had to take him to Kaiser to see a doctor. Once he'd seen the doctor, the x-ray was done and they found nothing. I had to take him back to school. As soon as I got home, I was on the phone again with Kaiser. Seems like all day I've been pulled in many directions. It's now 3:30 and I have to do the work that I've not yet finished. At 6 I have to go to my son's school to see his play. I'm already tired. I can't imagine what nourishment, fulfillment or fortification would like at this point. I feel deflated. There are still a few hours left. Maybe I will pull it off.

12/8 — 8:45pm

Yeah, today was a stream of frustrations, moving from one thing to the next, no connection to the activity, just feelings of overwhelm, resentment, and disconnection. I didn't do anything in the fulfillment category, the nourish category, or the fortify. I feel anxious, overwhelmed, mad at myself. I have zero connection to Mark these days. I feel like I have so many knots to untangle. I can see that in a day like today, simple gestures seem to dissolve, dissipate, and become unattainable. :-(Tomorrow is another day.

12/9 — nourish, fulfill, fortify — day 3 — 8:13 pm

Well, overall, there were some pluses and minuses. First thing, before the day got away, I took a walk outside. It was cold but before the train started rolling, I did what I needed to do. Walks are different than the gym, in some ways I perceive them as more nourishing—out with nature, I get a chance to clear my head, a chance to breathe, so it was good. As for the other 2: I had very slight fulfillment. I worked on this project for University of Portland, curating Brian Doyle essays for his final collection. I reached a point in the project where I can see the effort taking shape. That in itself was fulfilling. There was no fortification. I don't think there was time/interest/bandwidth to make it all come together. Observations are that this takes focus and intention. I'm out of touch with my Self most of the time. Last night I was alone. Mark was gone, Ethan was at his play. Without all the distraction, there was mostly a wellspring of emotion. Some of it was sadness. I feel so lost. I'm vague on how to fulfill or fortify. Nourishment seems easier or more straightforward, with exercise, water, healthier eating. But fulfillment and fortification, those are a mystery.

12/11 — nourish, fulfill, fortify — 6:51 am

I fell asleep last night before I had a chance to reach out. I met a friend for dinner for her birthday, came home, was full and tired, and fell asleep with my clothes on before doing anything (like brush my teeth, LOL) Yesterday the topic of self-care was not thought of; not in a resentful way, but not in a focused way. I got swept up in my busy-ness. I did nothing from the 3 categories, although seeing a friend I hadn't seen in a long time was minorly fulfilling. I definitely don't spend enough time with friends, I realized that. This whole self-care thing is going to have to be a matter of laser focus and intention. That was where it was left. Onward with this day.

12/11 — nourish, fulfill, fortify — 9:05 pm

Today was busy, and in the categories, here's what I know. Fortify: did nothing, fulfill: had some success with a work project that was fulfilling, nourish: the only category I made an effort in. I'd gotten this green vegetable powder mix. It tasted nasty but I drank it. Everything else is happenstance. I'm still slacking and I may be for a while, but I am at least doing some things. I know I will snap into place one day soon.

12/12 — nourish, fulfill, fortify — 9:07 pm

I was just about to go to sleep and I realized I hadn't reached out. I was in bed and truly thought I'd blow it off, but here I am. Nourish: ate oatmeal in the morning instead of toast. But that is all. No gym :-(Fulfill: been interviewing a guy who survived Hurricane Irma to pitch a story to some magazines about his family. Hearing his story and being part of this is fulfilling. Fortify: this is the one I can't seem to get to. I don't even know what this means. Maybe I need to rethink this goal or intention, or at least what I think it means and how I define it. I'm barely hanging on here with my intentions, but there's still a pulse. May take a while for the coma to end, but I will keep the pulse pulsing!

12/13 — nourish, fulfill, fortify — 9:14 pm

Hello. :-) I did one nourishing thing today and that was to put a "super greens" scoop of powder (it's new, I'm trying it) and a scoop of collagen into a shake with frozen strawberries and yogurt. It was an intentional step to do something healthy. I worked all day: super happy with where this Brian Doyle/University of Portland project is heading. It's going to be a showstopper. I can tell you that I am distant and avoiding this effort of showing up. All I can say is maybe a bit more time of giving these mediocre updates that have no real progress or grit. I am passing time and avoiding time all in one. Someday you'll get "the" report. The break-through, the real effort, the showing up. I am not down for the count, still hanging in, looking forward, not ready, but know it's gonna happen sooner than later. Happy Channukah!

12/14 — nourish, fulfill, fortify — 6:56 pm

I knew I had to check in. Every day seems the same. Although I did do something fortifying today. I went to Marylhurst to look into graduate school. I met with admissions and the head of the education depart-ment. So that was fortifying. Other than that, I'm a slug. I hide, avoid, divert, ignore, and have no time of silence without distraction. Am I lazy? Afraid? Don't want to get uncomfortable? I am impossible. :-(

12/16 — nourish, fulfill, fortify — 7:25 am

I had lunch with an old friend named John. He and I have known each other for 20 years. He had some interesting insight when I talked to him about my book project, why I feel stuck, why I don't move forward. He suggested I start by writing about why I can't write. Rather than it being something I am telling or sharing, make it an inquiry. I understood what he was saying and that was helpful. Does it nourish? Fortify? Fulfill? I'm not sure but I feel like my lunch with him does a little of all 3. I've always felt connected to him on an emotional, philosophical, intellectual level. We have rich conversations about things. Always have. I think what transpired out of the conversation may help me as I dig my way out.

12/16 — nourish, fulfill, fortify — 10:52 pm

Can I find it? What the hell is it? Mystery question for the day.

12/17 — nourish, fulfill, fortify — 5:23 pm

I just got home from working all day. I was at the graphic designer's house working on the Brian Doyle/University of Portland project. I left this morning at 9 a.m. and just got back. Ethan had gotten dropped off at noon, he was at his dad's for the weekend. So, he's been home for 5 hours. I call Mark on the way home from Camas and ask what Ethan's doing. He gets upset and says, "What do you think?" Apparently Mark had asked Ethan for help, Ethan didn't help, it pissed Mark off. Because this is an ongoing issue, I try to run interference, it doesn't help, so when I get home, there's instant stress. I walk into the kitchen. Dishes are piled up, the trash is piled up (both Ethan's jobs), Ethan is playing video games and Mark is going off on Ethan. My cat's hungry and begging me for food, and I just want to run away. I had imagined taking Ethan out for dinner, spending some time with him, but he's done nothing. I'm working with him about following up on expectations. This has been the tug-of-war struggle with Ethan the last few months. I can't see anything nourishing. I can't see anything fortifying. I can't see anything fulfilling, although working on the Brian Doyle project earlier was good. Within 5 minutes I am in a vortex.

12/18 —fortify — 8:40 pm

Sometimes I think with all the stuff that's going on—the seemingly constant barrage (more than usual?)—that building up my fortitude (as in emotional and physical health) would be more important to be able to withstand it all. I need to have the inner fortitude to face and deal with change. This stuff with my mom and her impending move, changing every minute and driving me nuts, the crazy politics, I've got to be stronger to withstand it all. I had a moment today where I could see that all this could quickly become a quicksand of depression, or fear, or anxiety. Life is overwhelming and big and ever changing. Sometimes I feel small in it all. I also had another depressing thought. This period feels like the time I'll look back on and say, "Yep, that's when I started to become invisible. That's when I slipped away into no longer being seen by the world or myself." I don't want that to happen. I don't want to look tired, or worn, or unhealthy, or fat, or unrecognizable to myself. I don't want to slip into the invisibility. Fortitude.

12/19 — nourish, fulfill, fortify — 9:13 pm

Thought a lot about fortification today. I feel so exposed to the world, fragile, so unprotected from the vastness of it all, so I thought about what fortification means. I have a hard time giving exact description to what I think it means, but I do know what I'm feeling when I say what fortification would feel like insides: strength isn't the exact word, neither is fulfilled. It's more like the idea of the inner constitution of something. The thread of continuity and alignment throughout (and as I write this, I imagine a motion of pointing to the top of my head and waving my hand up and down to describe this). It's interesting to try and understand and think about what's going on inside, while being an observer and yet, not really in it, in either instance.

12/21— nourish, fulfill, fortify — 6:47 pm

Once the holidays get closer, time moves in a strange cycle. Hours blend, productivity wanes. I'm going to try and stay motivated over the next few days to get shit done around the house still. My office, getting it organized, trying to get in the mindset for the new of the new. I have flashes of wanting to burst out; I can do this . . . be new, be brave, be active, be free . . . I have flashes of wanting to hibernate. Sleep, sedentary. Never the same feelings twice, yet always the same. I swim in a shallow pool of familiarity and am unable to break out. I wasn't connected to much of anything today; going through the motions. No nourish. No fortify. Fulfill? I'm lost in all of this.

12/22 — nourish, fulfill, fortify — 9:26 pm

Hello :-) Today was ok, I suppose. I was unmotivated to take care of some things, loose ends, which required going to Office Depot, the post office, Dollar Store. And rather than wait to do those things, I did them first thing in the morning. Sometimes mustering up motivation when I have none is tough, but I was able to pull that out this morning. I worked some. Then watched *The Marvelous Mrs. Maisel* with my son. I've seen the series twice already. If you've not seen it, wow! It's amazing. Today a little sad, a little overwhelmed. The news, racism, politics, the destruction of our education system. We're all drowning. Hanging on and hanging in.

12/24 — nourish, fulfill, fortify — 8:04 pm

Good morning. Hope you're doing something fun or with family the next few days. Overall: I got a few things done. Started the process of my office, which I'd been procrastinating on. It qualifies as fortifying. The category I lack the most, clearly, is the nourish. Day after day, nourish is the last to be addressed, if at all. Interesting to notice.

12/25 — nourish, fulfill, fortify — 8:26 pm

Hi there. Hope you ate some good food today, hung out in your pajamas or did something fun. I did do something nourishing today. I took a walk. Even though I didn't feel like it, it was good that I did. I always feel better when I walk. Gets me out of my head. It wasn't a long walk, but it was out of my warm pajamas and out of my warm house and into the elements. I did that in the morning. It was one of the first things I did. I realize that the nourishment piece is critical if I can do it first and get it out of the way.

12/27 — nourish, fulfill, fortify — 7:19 am

Oy, I was doing so well. Last night the obligation, or the self-expectation of reaching out to you, didn't even cross my mind. :-(How easily it goes away . . . When it comes to nourishment, fortification, or fulfillment, the holidays and lack of routine don't help. Pretty soon I'll be out of excuses, LOL.

12/27 — nourish, fulfill, fortify — 9:57 pm

Hello and good evening. Thoughts for the day: I think it's great I have these words—nourish, fortify, fulfill—meant to invoke motivation or action. But really, I have no vision about what I want my life to look like. This is a problem. The words to fill this life, to do this life, to inspire this life have no motivation or endgame without the vision. That's what I've come to today.

12/29 — nourish, fulfill, fortify — 8:35 am

Yesterday was uneventful, although I had a couple back-to-back interesting dreams. One was that I was about to get stuck under a train and was trying to figure out how to avoid getting run over. The one that followed? I had gotten contact info for a woman at a publishing house. I called and got the 411 on how to send a book proposal. I had that feeling of excitement, anticipation, hope about writing it and getting started—a feeling I haven't had in my waking life in a long time. So there's that. Interestingly, I get the bursts of wanting to move ahead, get rolling, but there's like a constipation of energy. I feel so blocked. I think this is what I need to ask for/meditate on: freeing the energy.

12/29 — nourish, fulfill, fortify — 6:04 pm

Hello and shabbat shalom :-) Because I'm going out again and might be home late, I will do this now. Today I did two things I'd consider fortifying and along the lines of what I imagine I want and will do more of. First, I wrote book content. It was a struggle, but I spent a chunk of time in this effort. Second, I watched a documentary about Queen Elizabeth. I knew nothing about her and so I took the curiosity and turned it into an education about a piece of history. I'm happy with these two things. Still not thinking about the nourishment component, but I know I will have to after the holiday mayhem.

12/30 — nourish, fulfill, fortify — 7:17 pm

Thanks for listening. Today I did a few things I consider productive. First, I went for a walk in the morning. Took care of the nourish thing. Next, met a good friend I haven't seen in a while; I consider this fulfilling. On the fortification front, probably the largest effort. I bought an online course from Jen Sincero about breaking bad habits; it's a 21-day online video and writing course. I like her style. Other than emailing you daily, which is huge as something for accountability, I have nothing else. If

I'm going to make these bold moves forward, I mean really make them, I have to set up the accountability piece. Not too much, but enough to provide parameters. So all in all, I'd say it wasn't a fruitless day. I am not necessarily feeling inspired, but I'm not necessarily feeling useless, either.

12/31 — 9:40 am

(a poem I wrote)

2017 adios

can't say that I loved you,

can say time will tell what you brought to teach;

can't say you were easy,

can say you were merciful;

can't say you were kind,

can say you were honest;

can't say you were smooth,

can say you were traversed;

can't say you were subtle,

can say you were alive

with transition, uncertainty, disgruntled by illusion.

May not have loved you every day,

May not have loved you every way,

May not be sad to see you go,

But blessedly, can say thank you,

at least I'm here,

and breathing in the dissatisfaction above the ground

and can thank you,

Thanks to you.

Hummingbird,
Don't Fly Away

One late winter day, Portland's first sun-filled sky of spring had arrived. Residing in soggy Oregon, the first sunny day after an epic wet-weather streak feels like a national holiday. The brilliant blue canopy sky dazzled. Golden daffodils were in bloom. Robins gathered twigs for nests.

That morning Mark went to Home Depot. He bought stuff for a sink repair. Perhaps the promise of spring had sprung on him, too. In the bag were two bird feeders: one for birds such as robins and blue jays, one for hummingbirds. I didn't think much of the feeders, other than it would be nice to see some nature around the yard. He also got birdseed and red hummingbird juice mix.

My husband is the guy who never follows a recipe. Though most times the end results are good, I could tell his hummingbird water and nectar concoction wasn't right. I went online to see if I could figure out the appropriate ingredient ratios. Thank goodness I did! I discovered that store-bought red nectar is poison for hummingbirds. The dye in colored nectars is red dye 40, made from petroleum.

Hummingbirds consume roughly 25 percent of their diet from nectar, including flowers. The rest of their nutrition comes from tree sap, insects, and pollen. Hummingbirds' fast breathing rate, rapid heartbeat, and high body temperature require that they eat often to meet the needs of their metabolism. Which is why what they put into their tiny bodies matters.

In fact, hummingbirds, while in flight, have the highest metabolism of all animals. Their heart rate can reach as high as 1,260 beats per minute, with a breathing rate of 250 breaths per minute—even at rest. (For more totally cool hummingbird facts, visit my website, www.memyselfie-andeye.com).

The best nectar that resembles flowers is an ordinary homemade blend of one part regular white cane sugar to four parts water. Mark made a batch, filled the feeder, then hung it outside in front of the living room window. Within an hour, a tiny hummingbird showed up! I squealed with excitement, and like a hopeful shop owner who had just opened for business, I called the bird our first "customer." From then on, all subsequent visitors to the feeders were known as customers.

Until then, I don't recall ever in my life observing a hummingbird up close. Its wings were moving so fast they were nearly invisible. Its beak was a needle. It was so adorable and tiny! Without hesitation, like a cupid's arrow through the heart, I instantly fell in love.

After the little bird darted away, I found myself eagerly staring out the window, waiting for my next customer. About 10 minutes later another one appeared to flitter in front of the feeder. I felt giddy. I was mesmerized by how cute their incredibly miniature bodies were, contrasted with their extreme agility.

Over the next few days it was hard to concentrate on a small writing project I had. I gravitated toward the hummingbird feeder, waiting for my new little friends to make appearances. I wanted to know everything about them: how they migrate, how they sleep, what they eat. The more I learned, the more I was drawn in. Mark was happy that I was smiling again.

As a business woman whose life had been measured by preparation, I felt out of my element, silly even, for having an unexplainable fascination that I didn't initiate. Nothing before had inspired me as much. I joined a Facebook group called Hummingbirds Anonymous, which is a resource site about feeding and care of the tiny birds. It has 50,000 passionate members worldwide.

I discovered that if you're around hummingbirds enough, they become familiar with you and eventually you can use hand-held feeders. There was an unexplainable connection I felt to hummingbirds. A kinship. In addition to family pets, I know some people feel this way about dolphins, elephants, or horses. Some characterize these kindred creatures as spirit animals. I'd never felt this before.

To make myself known, I sat outside on the deck for hours. I observed them in flight as they darted around the trees in our yard. I was willing to establish trust without a single expectation of what would happen. The strange thing was that these moments were the first time in years that I had just sat, doing nothing other than watching hummingbirds fly and spring clouds drift by.

Previously, because owning a business engulfed my time, I felt incredibly conflicted or guilty if I did nothing.

One afternoon, while sitting on the deck waiting for a hummingbird to appear, without my knowing or doing anything, I realized that I was content. I felt a joy I'd not felt for a long time. It was a joy I had done nothing to create.

I reflected on how long I'd lived without simple joy. How long I'd struggled to impose circumstances attached to expectations. I could see how I'd been so tied to being productive that what I did defined who I was, and thus, how I ultimately experienced life.

Right then I heard the familiar whirr of a hummingbird and it promptly appeared. There, less than six inches away from my face, the hummingbird hovered. My heart raced. Though its wings were beating as fast as propellers, its shiny, emerald-green body was completely still. A bright pink throat reflected in the sun.

I looked into its eyes and in return it stared deeply into mine. Amazingly, I could clearly tell he was as curious about me as I was about him. The hummingbird floated closer, slowly, and hovered only three inches away, at eye level. I stayed completely still, though my heart pounded. Our eye-to-eye contact remained fixed. We had the wildest instant of connection. I felt it and it was real.

Peering into the eyes of a curious hummingbird, I absorbed an affirming assurance. Awareness flooded in about *being* without *doing*, and embracing the unexplainable. I could accept the idea that sometimes happiness didn't have to derive from anything I did or created, but could be received through the smallest gift of connection.

* * * * *

Before long, my excitement spilled over into picking up a camera to see if I could capture in a frame what I felt in the presence of these beings. Thousands of photos later, I made adjustments to the aperture, speed, and lighting settings. Day by day, week by week, and month by month, my photos got better. Hummingbird images transformed from blurry blobs into luminescent displays of frozen wings.

Taking hummingbird photos helped propel me out of the darkness. It began a conversation about *being* without *doing*, and encouraged access to an entire other Me. Hummingbirds were little portals of access to who I once *was* and who I was *becoming*. They flew between my realms: the thinking/expectation/productivity identity I'd always known, and a barely familiar manifestation of the Me that dwelled deeper, within a heart-centric/unexplained/uninitiated place. Captured images served as translators between the two.

I reviewed my photographs at the end of each day. Some were truly beautiful. I wondered how I ended up with a technical capacity to capture them. As an amateur flower and landscape photographer, being able to stop the wings of a hummingbird mid-flight through the split-second trigger of a lens was exhilarating.

When I looked at pictures I'd shot, what I saw was *love*. Their little spirits conveyed a range of emotions through different poses and expressions. Love brought the ultimate belonging forward and guided our interactions. My fascination invited me to discover what hummingbirds represented.

Hummingbirds are signs of good luck, wisdom, and magic. If a hummingbird comes to find you—as in spiritually find you—it represents awakening. A hummingbird's fluttering wings move in an infinity pattern that conveys steady, seamless flow. They appear to share messages about life's continuity and the perseverance that is emblematic of life itself. They signify internal resilience and energy. Joy and adaptation. Magic and motion. All of which I was lacking and hungry for.

The synchronicity of the hummingbirds appearing and my having such an unexplainable connection to them was perplexing. In the throes of my Dark Flight, a magical fairy bird showed up to soften me. A tiny, resilient, living thing that was *magical because of flight*—how fast it flew, the multiple directions it flew, and the amazing things it could do because of its unique wings.

Because of what these creatures represented spiritually and the unencumbered joy they brought, plus an ability to capture them photographically that I have no idea how to explain, the hummingbirds became translators. They spoke from "me" to "Me."

They led me to traverse the terrain between my old identity's self based on thoughts, expectations, and judgment, and the Self trying to find its voice within Me. A Self delicately formulating within my heart, that could ultimately *be* in a moment without having to *do* anything to get there.

My "doing" self thought my interest and unexplained energy around this topic was silly. My budding relationship with hummingbirds, that I had done nothing to prompt, was irrational and made me uncomfortable. Yet every day, the harder it became to deny that *something* beyond my comprehension was transpiring. The contrasts and complements of where I was, who I was, and what I needed to move forward were becoming profoundly clear.

Perhaps when we do things, like paint, or write, or take photos of hummingbirds, we're trying to reach a Self that dwells within. Pictures of hummingbirds come from somewhere I can't explain. I just know that I love the moment they occur and can appreciate that moment as I review photographs I've taken. I experience joy again.

Somehow, such an innocuous thing proved to show a lot, do a lot, give a lot, and become a lot on the Flight of seeing my Self again. There was nothing I did to discover this, nothing I initiated. This leads me to wonder, if it was hummingbirds for me, what might it be for you?

Is there something that makes you happy without having to initiate or produce it? Is there an activity or circumstance that brings you simple joy? That isn't contingent on an outcome? Are there activities you do that feel silly?

I was embarrassed by how much joy I felt over the hummingbirds. Thanks to my new obsession, my friend joked she was going to change my name to Myrtle and buy me a puffy-paint sweatshirt with a hummingbird on it. I cruised the hummingbird forums, bought the wind chimes, set up the garden outside. But those little magical birds swept me right up. Taking pictures was icing on a joyously simple cake and was one of the first tangible windows into my heart. The act spoke to me in an unfiltered language. The result of my hummingbird photos tells me so. (To see some of the images, visit www.memyselfieandeye.com.)

Why do these unblemished parts of a Self get so buried? When our walls of stuff, and people, and expectations, and busyness, and identities start to crumble, there we are. Exposed and afraid. It's no wonder we fall apart. The matter of what's there, the density, is too much.

If you think about everything in a life that covers you up—all the moments, thoughts, interactions, disappointments, dreams, and ideas—the Self becomes like a lost fossil at the archaeological site of a lost civilization. Generations of people and families and stories get buried, one on top of the other. Your life, your experiences, your ultimate identity is comprised of all the generations of people, families, stories—all of it—everything that encompasses a time and place that's been left behind to be forgotten.

Sometimes it's a fluke that a passerby stumbles upon a subtle clue (a bone or relic) that indicates there's something beneath. In the case of identity, everything that it encompasses becomes its own lost civilization. The many selves we form and re-form ultimately create facades of who we are in order to adapt and survive.

This notion also leads to why I think social media is deceptive. Thousands of data bits and posts and likes and interactions are dirt and debris that cover and bury the glimmers of a Self's existence. We're too busy managing, handling, dictating, coercing, corralling a whole other Self that's projected out into the world every day.

By midlife, clues to who we are are too small, there's been too much time, too many thoughts, too many judgments, too many expectations that bury us. To find that lost civilization of a Self that was there before identity took over, the exterior of who we think we are needs to be blasted. Who's got energy to dig even a little, let alone the time to excavate, when living to survive has become a full-time job?

Judgment, the Dance &
a Butterfly Effect

February 2018.

I'm glued to a wall watching a room full of dancing people. The scene of rump shakers gone wild would be fine for a bar mitzvah or nightclub. But it's neither a shindig nor Studio 54. This jumble of gyrating flesh is in Embassy Suites Ballroom C, cutting a rug to George Michael's "Freedom" while in the zone of an "ecstatic dance." Meanwhile, I'm human adhesive.

The ecstatic dance is an intentional exercise capping off Day Two of a three-day Lee Harris Energy Mastery workshop. Instruction given: No talking during the hour-long dance. To anyone. The point of the dance is to be with one's Self, within one's space, to engage the physical body, to shake off energy accumulated from the day, to express the emotions of the body through the nonverbal form of creative dance.

The songs playing aren't as esoteric as one might imagine. Not that I'd heard the term ecstatic dance before, but if I had, my mind might have drifted to new-age flutes or Jew's harp. In this version, the Lee Harris ecstatic dance, Prince, Whitney, Boy George, and Stevie Wonder command the floor. The room is dark. To encourage movement, purple and pink disco lights flash to the beat.

I grew up in Los Angeles. Dancing, underage clubs, and Donna Summer are part of my DNA. I have no problem being alone or among strangers on a dance floor. Yet, this situation, these dancers, this expectation and purpose, are different. I've morphed into a pimply tweenage boy hovering around the punch bowl at a winter formal. I'm stiff, awkward, suctioned to a wall.

I gaze as ribbons of bodies sway and shimmy, arms glowing pink and purple from the lights as they fly, elbows swinging high in the air, faces blissed out by the beat, lost to liberation, eyes closed yet seeing *something*—a freedom, an awareness, a comfort within their own skin—that's a million miles away.

It's not seventh grade shyness stopping me from riding the disco train. I'm doused in judgment. But I don't yet understand that that's what has my body as fixed as concrete.

Through the standing speaker near my head, Annie Lennox belts out, "Sweet dreams are made of this . . . " I think, *Who is she to disagree?*

I travel the world
and the seven seas,
Everybody's looking for something . . .

Annie called it. Aren't 75 people dancing alone, together, a testament that we're all looking for something?

A flash of self-consciousness wonders if anyone looking for something notices the frigid, middle-aged, wall-dwelling shadow? I sigh.

Everyone else is at ease.

Everyone is free.

In their bodies.

Why am I so awkward?

Why can't I *be* with myself?

Or own my body?

A lump in my throat spits a couple of tears down each cheek. I'm trapped; I tell myself how ridiculous I am—it's simply dancing. What am I so afraid of? Why can't I just move?

A woman in front of me goes for it. She's an unashamed full-bodied woman, maybe in her late 20s. She swivels her feet, taps her knees, sways robust hips pendulum wide. She's buxom and "the girls" resoundingly bobble, her head rolls 'round and prompts cream-colored hair tendrils to flitter through blinking lights, like a swirl of magenta and violet butterflies. I envy her untethered confidence as music inspires her to swim in the pool of her skin.

Meanwhile, I drown beneath my sinkhole. I've separated my Me from being immersed in an unfolding experience. My head questions inaction, yet my body's paralyzed to dive. Everyone's having fun, splashing through movement, without words, without structure, without expectation.

Without judgment.

There. I said it.

That's when I realized.

I've danced a thousand times before . . .

Judgment.

It sneers: *Don't do it, you'll look silly; this is stupid. What would people see if they peered in? Are those people dancing a bunch of freaks? Would my husband or children think I've finally lost it? Is this—the activity, the energy weekend—just a bunch of woo-woo bullshit?*

Yet here I am. I am contradiction and so is the moment. If I'm ever to get closer to my Self, my being, my body is the portal. I've never been connected to or comfortable with my body. It's stayed a separate matter. I have to acknowledge the blockade—the thing that keeps me on the outside, pressed to the wall, away from the moment while others delight—as Judgment.

I've not seen Judgment before as it relates to my Self. Sure, I've been critical. *I'm sick of being fat. How did I let myself go? Why can't I change?*

I might claim to have opinions about things. Lots and lots of opinions about *everything*. But these are not the same as Judgment, at least in the context of my Self.

I've never before been aware of Judgment in my own life—sneaky little judgments disguised as passing thoughts. I wasn't aware that I had an unspoken relationship with Judgment so closely associated with how I move, or don't move, in the world.

If I stay frozen and indulge Judgment about how I look or why this is stupid, what do I give up? If I don't dance right now, I may never swim beneath the surface of my emotional pool or do things in spite of discomfort. If I judge all of it, then fuck it, I don't have to explain why I never put my Self into a moment. I already solved that.

If I ignore it, and dance anyway, Lord help me. I'm stripped. I can't explain why the thought of it leaves me feeling so exposed, but that's what it is. Flip on a blinding spotlight, I'm naked. Without Judgment, I have no protection from emotional transparency. Yet I know on an intrinsic level, the emotional galaxy—that vast terrain beyond my thoughts and judgments and opinions and fears—is where my not-yet-discovered brightest stars shine.

I've yearned for years to be nearer to the elusive places within my Self that I truly don't know; the aspects of my being that are mysteries disconnected. The complete stranger to me within that is *Me*. The certainty of deeper shadows that are closer to my soul or essence or heart (I'm not sure what to call it) that I've believed are there, yet remain obscure like untraceable black holes within a foggy nebula. And similar to unrealized aspects of one's Self, I know deeper truths exist, just as black holes do.

I've been galaxies away. For a long time.

Midlife grief, disillusionment, and the very complexity of being lost have to shift. If I could just break though mental barriers that are so thick, so dense, and reach out—bust through not understanding *how* to shove myself closer to places nearer to a *Me* that lurks beneath and that scare me.

I can't *not* know anymore. The cost of not knowing is at the expense of fulfillment. How will I unearth what I can become or unfold Janna, a person I've always known, yet don't know, who's been given a treasure of being alive, if I'm stuck to a wall—imaginary, or in this case, for real?

I see my Self out there, somewhere, on a dance floor. She's uncluttered. It's *Me* and I watch it from a distance unable to float toward it.

This moment is one I can't pass up. I recognize how much joy I'm depriving my Self by hugging a wall. The significance of inaction and consequence don't escape inadequate, naive, hopeful *Me:* I *have* to make a move. The only way through to whatever awaits beyond discomfort is to pry myself away from the wall and push toward the center of the floor. Not on an edge, not on the side, I gotta go where there's no denying.

I'm terrified. My palms sweat, my heart pounds, I feel stupid, I imagine I'd rather be in a dentist's chair getting a root canal. Yet, I want to take it in—authentic freedom and simple collective joy. I need to take it in. I'm desperate to rewrite an outcome of watching it all dance by.

Then, Chaka Khan's "Ain't Nobody" chimes in like a talisman . . .

Captured effortlessly
That's the way it was
Happened so naturally
I did not know it was love
The next thing I felt was you
Holding me close
What was I gonna do?
I let myself go . . .

Her velvet murmur lulls my spirit toward another place. Another time. Her invocation resurrects a younger, immaculate Me . . .

And now we're flyin' through the stars
I hope this night will last forever . . .
Ain't nobody (nobody)
Loves me better (better)
Makes me happy
Makes me feel this way . . .

Then, in the midst of her melody, Chaka whispers through ballroom airwaves, *Go on girl, it's your time to jump . . .*

Through the current of bodies, guided by finesse, *Ain't nobody loves me better, makes me happy, makes me feel this way,* I stiffly dance my way within the labyrinth of elbows and arms. Although I'm a starched collar, my legs and arms find mobility.

No one witnesses while everyone witnesses a milestone of Me, as I land in the center. I thank Chaka for the lift.

Wow! In the center, I become the head of a pinwheel. The surrounding rush of twirling air is warm from bodies in flow. The heat of the lights and the tempo are hypnotic. I can't recall tasting such collective bliss; together, people are liberated from thought, expectation, and Judgment, united by simple expression and joy. *This* is what community feels like. The revelation is amazing.

Have you ever been in the middle of a dance floor and absorbed the rushing heat from life-affirming motion spiraling around you?

Just as quickly as my senses allow awareness as a reward for braving the center, my mind fights to kick it out. *This is so stupid.* I lash back, *Stay out of my head. Don't think about who's watching.* I want to give in and linger with the sensation of wonder. As thought and feeling spar, the song changes and I emphasize my step to Whitney's "I Wanna Dance with Somebody." How about Me? Can I dance with Me?

Aware that both realities seek control, I ask myself, *Is it possible to feel joy and freedom at the same time I'm experiencing hesitation and judgment? If I'm uncomfortable, conflicted, and struggling to let go, can I concede that these two different experiences can both be true at the same time?*

Thankfully, the makeshift treaty's enough to keep my feet flowing. I acknowledge these steps as tender.

* * * * *

Several questions from the experience became clear: Why did I ever call on Judgment at all? Why did it remain hidden and strengthen over the course of my life until the absurd pinnacle I'd reached: 50 years old, stuck to a ballroom wall, avoiding an ecstatic dance during an energy healing workshop, surrounded by a swirl of freer-than-me spirits whose physical liberation I envied so much it made me cry?

Who knew the center held a key?

Who imagines that one day they'll contemplate such a preposterous scenario?

A few days later, I dealt cards of insight onto my Self's table with regard to my avoidance of dancing toward the center. Here was the hand:

Over the course of many years, Me and Judgment developed an unspoken arrangement. The two entities reinforced their co-existence as it slipped in unnoticed. When emotional experiences (that might have brought closeness to a deeper place within) were potentially too heartfelt, Judgment became protective. Responses such as *Don't do that; People will think . . . ; That's stupid; You look silly* evolved into a coating, an armor, a distraction, an alias . . . all to fool a predator of raw emotion.

Judgment upholds, *Why not merely bypass it all?*

Judgment appears as discernment or opinion or a barrier to the full breadth, depth, or access to any given moment. It warns of feeling silly, uncomfortable, awkward, but doesn't give a reason. Rather than providing explanation or prompting any honest internal process for evaluation, it goes into deflection and makes external embarrassment or discomfort the star of the show. It skips over emotional evaluation (how *could* this experience make me feel?) and masks itself as instinct.

Huh.

What a trippy discovery.

Final thought: Self-criticism or opinion is the perpetual *mental* narrative about my life that keeps tabs on the surface of my experiences. It's chatter in my mind that has its own sense of purpose; if I tell myself I look fat or ask why I haven't gone to the gym, I have something that is to be done, or not done, that I can name and feel bad or good about.

Self-criticism or opinion relates to "doing" in the world. It has nothing to do with "being" per se, the foreign terrain of emotions that are what they are; though I try and prove otherwise, that there's nothing to be done about emotions . . .

Judgment is an *emotional* barrier—it diverts access to living any emotion too deeply before raw feelings of loss or hope are given a chance. Judgment prevents the "being" in life. What if I let go and danced? What is the hesitation of loosening self-control and allowing a sense of freedom? Does a glimpse of liberation conflict with my daily m.o. of maintaining control?

These ideas can be confusing, so I'll conclude with an analogy. Judgment is life's condom: it governs protection and tightly clings. Outcomes will be sort-of sensations for life's pleasure and friction and tension and inhibitions. It even subdues exploding excitement. Unlike a condom, however, it's not easy to snap off Judgment. Not when it's been around for as long as it has. Not when the emotional stakes of its absence and subsequent exposure seem so high.

I'm not sure where the new insight about my relationship with Judgment will lead me. Perhaps as I grow and notice more, dissolve layers of uncertainty, when I clamp during emotional discomfort, I can summon the purple and pink glow of Chaka's spirit and the ecstatic dance.

Although prying my Self from the wall to dance through a crowd of familiar strangers was uncomfortable, my time had come. Stay stuck or be free. Not know or know. Fly toward the center.

Once there, I stood in the center marveling. Fellowship and freedom to *be* swirled around Me. The rewards experienced ultimately derived not from my single act or the courage of getting there, but from the truce with Judgment—which momentarily allowed in the simple joy and cumulative effect of dancing butterflies.

Never Ever Gonna Write a
Book, Nope, Nohow

I was never going to write a book. There are a million of them out there. *Eh? What's the point? Who would care?* Yet a faint voice whispered about the importance of midlife identity grief and sharing what I'd learned. I'd jotted blurbs of observations during my Dark Flight but over the months I got sick of hearing myself whine. *Oh dear GAAWWWWD! Shut the hell up!!* So I did.

What was stopping me?

Judgment and Expectation conspired to earn my silence: *I have nothing of value to say. Nothing new to bring to the conversation. I don't "know" my voice. A book I wrote would never be good enough.*

The emotional realm is foreign. It's the other Janna, the unencumbered Self, the being sans identity projection, that is a total stranger. I was aware that it lurked, but its full existence wasn't visible until everything shattered. This is the Eye I'm learning to see.

The Eye in this context is the recognition that after an embedded identity suddenly explodes, there is an entire other Self, one that's untouched and precious and innocent and vulnerable and scary and awkward and hopeful. This awareness combines with the steps, process, and unfolding of rediscovering one's identity.

How and when midlife identities crash is something unique to each person, but I'm convinced the occurrence is common. A desire to help others navigate their own Dark Flights moved me forward. I brought up the book idea to Raphael. I shared that although I had the desire, every time I sat down to do it I got tongue-tied.

Judgment was on duty. *What if it don't get published, what about finding an agent, what do I have to say that is interesting, how would it get edited* . . . I had every possible outcome mapped out, weighing me down, preventing me from moving forward.

He suggested viewing the book merely as having a conversation with my Self. To take the pressure off potential outcomes (whether or not I'd get published), I could write whatever I wanted because as far as I knew, no one would see it.

This allowance removed stress and opened a doorway. Before, it was impossible to have a conversation because I wasn't aware that was what was needed. There was too much noise, too many expectations, too much fear. That way of recognizing a conversation prompted words from a different place. It bypassed the filters of judgment and expectation.

The allowance enabled insightful discoveries and to grieve identity losses I didn't even know I was sad about. It enabled me to laugh at my own ridiculousness. It's been a new awareness to tap into and feel, and to understand a portal to my Self that bypasses the filter of *me.*

A book was the *invitation* for conversation. For some, maybe it's cooking, or painting, or taking pictures, or drawing, or sewing. These allow expressions from a place within our Selves outside of what we identify with. Right around the time I explored the notion of writing a book purely for the sake of conversation, serendipity occurred to encourage a "yes."

You know how with Facebook feeds, there are friends of friends and people you've never met that are part of your cyber-sphere? As publisher of *Local Living* magazine, I'd amassed a lot of these people. Authors were among the mix. One author was Hope Edelman. Since my magazine dealt with issues related to families, at some point Hope's work as author of *Motherless Daughters* had come across my desk. Her book "examines the effects of the death of a mother on a woman's identity, personality, family and life choices."

One day in January 2018, Hope posted a message about coaching sessions for creative memoir writers. If I thought I was writing a memoir,

I would have said *forgettaboutit.* Memoir-worthy people have seen some shit, survived some shit, discovered some shit, or done amazing shit. I didn't fall into a memoir-worthy category. "Creative memoir," however, opened up the field enough for thoughts about what transpired in midlife, as a means to help others, as opposed to a story about me. I reached out to inquire about her services.

I've done a lot of writing over the years, but the majority has been observational and journalistic—the kind of writing that takes words as a third party and repackages them into other words to report on events or ideas that are removed from me. Hope's coaching facilitated dialog to sort out emotions from the thoughts, from the experiences, and importantly, from the writing process. We started the writing coaching process in February. We connected every other week for several months.

Topics explored included fear, grief, change, identity, loss, disappointment, and love. I thought and wrote a lot about these topics as pieces of dialog from an even larger ongoing conversation with my Self.

During a FaceTime session, Hope asked, "Is this book looking back on what you've learned, or are you still in the middle of it and taking people along the journey?" From her perspective, that answer informed the style and intent of the writing. It was a fair question. I had no answer.

Months later, after my Dark Flight began, this book, this conversation, became both. This identity shift that started by being leveled, that clipped my wings and thrust my spirit into a Dark Flight over unknown waters, was at a place of feeling fragile. But hey, after detonation, my heart was beating. I was past poking my head above ground and closer toward exploring my surroundings. I was seeking sparse radio signals as I heard them.

Do You Know the Way
to Santa Fe?

Based on daily disruptions that transpire throughout a single day in my house (think cats scratching doors to go in and out, husband jamming electric guitar in basement, kid yelling at Xbox), it was clear I'd never achieve the depth of internal dialog this assignment required. I tried to sit and write, but was drawn to every external distraction, on top of all the ways I distracted myself. Sitting still was difficult.

I thought about how people in the professional world take sabbaticals to re-evaluate their lives, wind down the day-to-day distractions, and in many cases use a block of time to write. Maybe that's what I would do. I couldn't financially afford being gone for a month or two as what I imagined a typical sabbatical to be, and I definitely didn't want to be away from my kids that long. Yet, a week seemed too short to achieve the goal of truly sitting with myself and listening. I settled on two weeks.

I thought about where I'd go, given that I didn't want to be alone in the woods without Wi-Fi and Kathy Bates *Misery*-level solitude (thanks, Stephen King!). I wanted to be inspired. Santa Fe, New Mexico, has always felt like home; I love the art, the sky, the clouds, the color of the earth. Plus it's easy to be alone without being cut off from civilization. I started looking into rentals. Casitas were relatively affordable.

With logistics handled, that left my hesitation and fear. I'd never truly been alone with my Self. I was terrified at the idea but couldn't pinpoint why. It felt like standing on top of the biggest ledge of a cliff, being asked to shuffle toward the edge until my toes dangled over, and then being instructed to look straight down. Even thinking about it now makes my stomach flop. That's the feeling that came from imaging myself alone for two weeks for the purpose of meeting my Self.

I deemed this my Grand Gesture. I came to the conclusion that when we're in the Dark Flight of the Self, we reach a point of being so lost that our identities are nowhere to be found—and as a result, we have to travel some hellacious internal spaces to greet our Selves at our most *uncomfortable* edges. We make a proclamation that screams "Hey! I'm over here!" and then take a tremendous plunge. Fear and all. Hesitation be damned. It's time. And the gesture's so emotionally grand—so spiritually jarring—that it can't be ignored.

I booked and paid for the airline ticket and casita for June on a credit card so I couldn't change my mind. It was March, which meant I'd have a couple of months to freak out, but I'd put my Grand Gesture into motion. I was going to Santa Fe to be alone for two weeks and stay in a little casita 10 miles out of town to do nothing other than converse with my Self. A few friends thought I was insane and mentioned how they could never do that. Others claimed outright envy.

* * * * *

I'm sitting outside on a lovely porch at the rented tiny yet affordable Airbnb casita, which is shrouded by faint scents of sagebrush, wet earth, and lavender. The clay-colored valley spills beneath the protective Sangre de Cristo Mountains, dotted by pinion and juniper. Large puffs of smoky clouds glide northeast. Up until this moment, I've been on the move, doing anything to avoid crawling out of my skin from the uneasiness of being still.

I walk over to the mini-library of books I've set up on the small table—a selection of 15 books I lugged from home in case my writing voice went mute (I had no faith that I would be able to come through) and I needed inspiration. I choose *The Power of Flow*. I step outside, place the "I (heart) Santa Fe" coffee mug on the wicker table, and settle into a rocker to contemplate the beautiful mountains.

I thumb through the book's introduction. The author has shared a story about a man who dreamt about moving to Colorado and although he firmly lived in Austin, within weeks everything in his life, in one serendipitous occurrence after another, had been turned upside down. Before he knew it, he was offered his dream job in Colorado. *Pfffff . . . really? Just like that, huh?*

My inner cynic is so annoyed, I shut the book. Sometimes these self-help spiritual books belong to everyone else. I've hardly related to many of the popular titles out there. (I'm talking to you, *Eat, Pray, Love.* Who the hell has the time or money to run off to Bali, Italy, and India? And yeah, she had no kids to disappoint by putting herself first). In fact, sugar-coated, solution-based books piss me off because stories of the journeys or discoveries never feel realistic or relatable to everyday people like me. Lessons are often prescriptive, neat, *Better Homes & Garden*-ish about the whole self-discovery mess. Other times, reading them would prompt me to believe I was on the wrong side of a Barnes & Noble track, the side that left me feeling more like shit, less aware, less evolved, and less fulfilled.

I feel exiled from the secret handshake or capacity for enlightenment and all the magical synchronicity that happens for everyone else *The Power of Flow* seems to be talking to. Deflated, I gaze back at the mountains and, like an untrained dog that needs redirecting, a gentle reminder to just sit pops into my head. I focus on the fragrant sagebrush. I hear the sweet chatter of birds. It's so beautiful here. I want to live here someday. Stillness seizes the moment. Unexpected tears overtake me. *Will I ever figure this out?*

As pent up emotions spill out, something almost unbelievable happens. In the middle of my tear stream (after I've just written how spiritual occurrences happen for others but not me) I hear a familiar whirr of wings. Less than three feet in front of me, on the tip of a bush that has beads of small purple flowers, a hummingbird appears! It floats and hovers like a loud bee. Recognizing that there are acres and acres of flower possibilities around this isolated property for this little one to have flown to, I can't believe what I am seeing.

So strange and lovely and perfect. If I had read of this happening in someone else's book, I'd have called bullshit. It was way too neat.

He hovers right in front of me for about 20 seconds. By the time I fully realize what's happening, he is halfway into his brief show. Then, as quickly as the magical coincidence becomes real, he zips away.

I am stunned about the timing—what I'd just written juxtaposed with what actually transpired. I sit in the rocker sipping cold coffee to make logic of something unexplainable.

*   *   *   *   *

Alone in Santa Fe, writing in dialog for hours and hours each day, for two weeks, I definitely had a strange yet real contact. Each day was pretty much the same. Wake up around 7 a.m. Make a cup of instant Maxwell House hazelnut coffee. Sit on the porch in the wicker rocking chair admiring the incredibly blue sky and the Sangre de Cristo Mountains. Contemplate how far from home I was. Think about my kids. Feel grateful for Mark. Sip more coffee. Make some oatmeal or have a yogurt. Stare at my laptop to avoid writing. Around 8 a.m., walk over to the tiny desk to sit down and start writing. Tell myself I can't get up until lunch.

It turned out that once I got out of my own way, words flowed. I'd take a small lunch break to make a sandwich. Then I'd go back to writing until about 5:30. I'd call it a day with a celebratory margarita at a nearby bar or restaurant. Stay until about 8 p.m. Go back to the casita and watch three hours of *Gilmore Girls* until I fell asleep.

Although I'd accomplished over 48,000 words, it wasn't the amount of words I came home with, but the *quality* of those words. I did feel as if I'd accomplished the goal of having a conversation with my Self. The words that appeared came from a different place—they weren't constructed from my mind but derived from a place deeper, a more untarnished heart-space within me. They were words, ideas, questions, and discoveries that my mind had never tapped into, at least in quite the same way, before.

The nature of the identity crash I speak of, a Dark Flight of the Self, isn't just that something unfortunate happens, like losing a job or getting divorced. Something does occur (from one of the Seven D's) that sets it in motion, but because we're at a specific midlife point, the occurrence is received in such a way that the rest of the pillars topple.

Somehow we're on a ledge. There's sadness, fear, and a willingness deep within to extend a hand and introduce ourselves to ourselves in a very different way, in a very new way, in a very real way. We've journeyed toward this precipice. We don't know how we arrived and we're not sure where we're going. We can't comprehend where all the moments leading up to this one have gone. Perhaps before this moment we weren't ready for the gift or responsibility or depth of what the Flight requires.

I don't think the steps I took to sit alone with my Self for two weeks were about courage. A friend once shared how brave I am. I don't think courage comes from the "doing," because as life happens, including our professional life and our roles as parents, or spouses, we "do" all the time. The "doing" is what we know and what gets reinforced.

What felt courageous was recognizing that everything I was "doing" wasn't who I was. Everything I was producing wasn't Me. All the stuff I had fabricated around my life were pieces of my life, but they weren't the core. They didn't comprise my identity.

My real courage came from braving this awareness and then feeling uncertainty. The bravery is in the aspects of the unfamiliar. It came down to the fact that I just had to know. I didn't want to go through the rest of my life *not* knowing.

An obvious question might be *How will I know when I know?*

Does the Dark Flight of the Self carry me toward something? Am I leaving part of me behind? It could be both. It could be neither. Over the two weeks in Santa Fe, I realized I hadn't taken time to grieve a Me that had been left behind. I hadn't taken a breath that was needed because I was too busy doing. We keep spinning and spinning and the more we spin, the more we need to spin. I was mentally overwhelmed and emotionally exhausted.

I had never been alone with my Self as an adult for a period of time. I had no idea what that would be like. I'd designated a time and place where I had nothing standing in the way between me and Me. Two weeks alone somewhere to fill my spirit and have a conversation with my Self was my Grand Gesture. I was terrified. That was my unfamiliar. That was my ledge.

Two weeks alone in Santa Fe provided an invaluable basis for what I'd been searching for. It affirmed hunches about a deeper Me. I got a glance into the whole other world of my Self. I could see her, I could talk to her, I could appreciate her, and I could allow what she had to say. Yet, this was still as an observer. Which was fine. After all, it was a starting point. We were just getting acquainted.

What I learned was that I wouldn't let my Self down. Strange to discover there really was another part of me, the me that is Me, that was hanging around waiting to interact. Those two weeks flew by. I enjoyed my own company. I came home confident that I was someone worth paying attention to. I felt that by braving something that had seemed insurmountable, a big fat ledge of discomfort, I'd accomplished something important. The mission of my Grand Gesture was complete.

My last night there, I watched the sun set and the puffy clouds soften to pink against a dimming turquoise sky. I absorbed the feeling that I was doing something grand by being there alone; by striking out into the unknown, and by having a conversation with my Self. Perhaps I understood that the surrounding mountains were big enough to embrace the buried grief and heartbreak.

There are four things a Self wants:

To be heard.

To be seen.

To be understood.

To be loved.

(Just Like) Starting Over

When I got home from Santa Fe at the end of June I was feeling inspired—about my discoveries and my capacities, and about this book/conversation with my Self that I'd committed to. July was meant to focus ideas I'd come up with and corral them into a formal book proposal. A book proposal is a document that summarizes what a book is about, has a sample chapter, and breaks down how the book will be marketed to make a prospective publisher money. It's a business plan to share with potential publishers and agents.

In August each year, Portland hosts a big literary event called the Willamette Writers Conference. For three days, there are dozens of workshops, notable speakers, and tons of networking. Hopeful writers across all genres can spend $35 dollars to schedule eight minutes to sling book proposals at prospective agents and publishers. I had scheduled three "pitch sessions," one with an acquisitions editor from a publishing house and two with agents, each of whom represented the category of "creative memoir."

My book was far from done, yet I was hopeful. I felt strongly about the message—identity crash in midlife (Dark Flight of the Self) as something more common than people share, authentically shown with its innate messiness, along with how true identity can evolve. I felt the work could be relevant to a large pool of struggling people. I had been on a mission to have a conversation with my Self. Along the way, I had realized I was also on a mission to help other lost midlife souls feel less alone.

With only four weeks to get the proposal together, July was hunker-down time. By the end of the month I was pleased with the content I'd shaped and compiled. I went shopping to pick out a power-professional outfit (I was too damn fat for all my others clothes!). The agent and publisher pitch appointments were scheduled for the first morning.

The day of the conference arrived. I mentally prepared for the first meeting as I walked into the ballroom at my designated time. I found the assigned table, introduced myself, and took a seat.

I was told by a female acquisitions editor from a publishing house that my title, "Me, My Selfie & Eye" wouldn't resonate with millennial readers and I should *strongly* consider changing it. She then asked (before I had a chance to tell her about the book's premise) how many followers I had on the various social platforms? When I could not claim 500,000+ followers on Instagram, her meager interest took an even steeper dive, and five of my eight minutes had already passed.

Aware time was ticking, I pointed out the section in the book proposal with the marketing strategy and audience development that was part of the plan. Without even taking a glance at it, she handed back my proposal and in a seasoned rejection voice, said, "Really, it's all about followers." And with that, my dud of a firecracker eight minutes were done.

The next two appointments were with agents. These pitches followed a similar trajectory—a proclamation that Platform is King! and that everybody is a nobody unless somebody has followers. I was disappointed. Not in myself, not in the outcomes, more in the fact that such superficial criteria dictate whose stories ultimately get published. Again, a reminder of the importance of the *projection* of who we are rather than who we *really* are. By way of example, Honey Boo Boo and Kim Kardashian both have book deals.

The rest of the day was spent checking out a few workshops, one of which was given by an agent about the tips and tricks to landing an agent. The more I heard about the hoops and red tape and drama and concessions involved, and the years it typically takes to get a book out into the world, the less interested I was in embarking on that road.

Another workshop was given by Steve Spatz, the president of Book Baby, a company that offers authors a self-publishing option. It highlighted why many authors choose this route—because of the creative control it offers authors, as well as the ability to revise text. They also provide access to distribution. I was looking forward to the idea of directly connecting with people, not with the idea of red tape. Self-publishing seemed the ideal option.

Post conference, I felt let down, after the hype leading up to it. My confidence in moving forward with *Me, My Selfie & Eye* had taken a hit. I had to unpack where the letdown was coming from. As I sifted through salvaged pieces of my confidence, I realized what it was. I was now 51 years old, and I was starting over. After everything I'd been through the last few years, that realization hadn't truly hit me.

The next few months, from August to October, I floundered. I'd had such an emotional high from Santa Fe, felt so confident and grounded, as if I'd made such strides. Now I was being sent back, way back, to the reality that I was at Square One. At 51.

I was in awe that during the years of the long Flight, the core of that thought never occurred to me. That was both depressing and liberating. On one hand, I was no longer who I was. I could welcome possibilities for my life. On the other hand, starting over is a big deal. It's like facing a mountain *and* a dragon. The setback enabled doubt to creep in.

Meanwhile, I had a small editorial project that kept me busy and I had been booked for a speaking engagement about midlife identity loss. But emotionally, I was hazy. I had no desire to write, I was unclear where the book needed to go. I struggled to find words. Things with Mark were estranged.

I was also reeling from my daughter Violet's recent move out of the house. She'd always been a source of comfort. My daughter felt like the heart of my home, metaphorically, and her absence rippled every day. She'd started taking classes at Portland Community College and had gotten a job at Starbuck's. Violet was truly branching out in her young adult life. She always had an extraordinary maturity and depth.

It was a lonely time. Since Mark and I hadn't been connecting at home, there was no dialog about the monumental change and my heartbreak over my daughter's exit. I understood she needed to do what she needed to do and I was proud of her for making her own decisions. Yet having my daughter move out was one of the most emotionally leveling things I'd been through. Talk about grief.

The next big event on the horizon that I was looking forward to was the Soul Magic retreat in Costa Rica in October that I had booked in February. Without the familiar comfort of my daughter at home, I felt aimless on top of aimless—entirely unneeded and invisible.

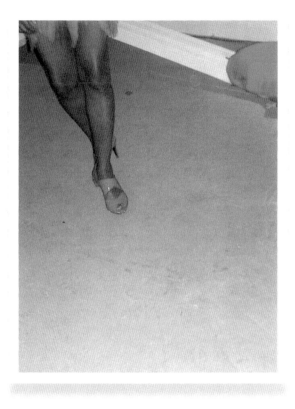

A Bear in My Woods

Several weeks before the big Soul Magic Costa Rica trip (booked that previous February), I'd been scrolling on Facebook one morning and came across a photo of a local Native American artist. He looked interesting and we had many friends in common. Sometimes I peruse profiles of artists or musicians to fill my cyber world with passionate creators. I look at their websites for inspiration. When I clicked on the weblink to his art, the link didn't work. I sent a message asking where I could find his art. From this greeting, a psychic connection to the bear—his spirit animal, as he proclaimed—was ignited.

I'd never cheat on my husband. However, it can be said that feeling seen is seductive. I'd felt invisible for a long time—unattached to and unaware of my Self. I hated looking at photos of me. I couldn't believe how fat and unrecognizable I'd become. Whether or not these things were true is inconsequential. I know how I saw me—like a fat fog huffing and puffing through her days just to catch her breath. I wanted to evaporate.

At first, "the bear" and I chatted about where we lived, the importance of art. Then he mentioned that I seemed interesting. He'd seen my hummingbird photos and asked about my connection to them. He sent a picture of himself holding a crow. I was intrigued by him as an artist, the poetic way in which he described himself. He followed a traditional Native lifestyle of no drinking, no smoking, no watching sports. He used his hands to make things, including art. He grew his own food. I had plenty of mental room to paint a picture.

Soon the chat with the bear took a turn. I was feeling the admiration of someone I'd never met. He sent me a seductive poem he'd written about the moon. None of it seemed real, actually, and the fact that a man seemed so attracted to, fascinated by, and interested in me was flattering. Although I wanted to float in the fantasy and thrill and excitement, I had my feet on the ground and in my marriage. But this was a strange, unexpected form of visibility. I could *feel* how much he wanted me.

Over the next few days as we chatted, he made it expressly known that he was interested in me. When he asked if there was someone in my life, I told him I was married. At the same time, my awakened desire to be seen was incredibly alluring. He seemed to have some knowing or insight or psychic hotline into my identity fragmentation and vulnerability. He asked, "Who is Janna today?"

(Picture the ridiculousness of this next *Desperate Housewives* scene: I lit some sage and switched Pandora to the Native American flute station as I sat at my desk to answer.) I responded, "Janna is the little girl running away from home to find her home. Janna is a daisy chain of contradiction: strong yet vulnerable; assured yet uncertain; all in her Self yet flung from her Self; aware yet naive; hopeful yet doubtful; Janna is being spun into some unknown circle of life as a thread, a fiber in the river of unfolding . . . Janna is in grief, in birth, in solitude, and in awakening . . . Janna is unknown yet more known than before."

With all the churning kundalini energy that had been awakened, my surprise at how good it felt to be seen and wanted in that way, a realization that I hadn't completely faded into midlife, I transferred the experience into words and off my mental, emotional, and spiritual plate. I wrote the following poem.

> If he appeared in a dream, he'd be forthright, mysterious, intriguing.
> He'd ask to see her. He'd make it known his eyes are open.
> She'd be skeptical of rapidly forming magic,
> and yet,
> She'd be thirsty, parched really, to be seen.

She'd wonder why all of what she'd questioned over what was
needed was being shown in a mirror of another.
A bear, no less.
A Native American symbol of protection, introspection,
and intuition.
A bear who dances with crows.
A bear of the land, of the spirit, of the ancestors, of
the seasons,
who communes with fish and sky and earth.

The bear would summon her,
a siren illuminated from her own shadow,
whispering, *Come out to play* . . .
traipse in the illusion of my woods,
dance within the falling leaves,

the bear growls, *I hunger to see you.*

She twirls in the leaves,
spins and spins and spins through breath of autumn's changing colors.
Dizzy, around and around, swirling,
sienna, crimson, pumpkin,
fall whirls in twirling light.

where is up,
where is North,
where is my home?

Did she summon the bear?
 Show me
She must have quietly begged a generous star

show me that I can still be seen
that I didn't disappear
that what my heart needs is not a lie
show me
that I'm awakening
not left behind

The bear whispered,

U ok with what's come about
Things yet to be defined
Maybe explored
In the name of inspiration?
U r an interesting creature
Fun
Smart
Beautiful
. . . Could be dangerous.

A flattering gust left the wind unsure of its own
sacred direction.

to the east, the wind was whisked by the hummingbird;
to the north, patience and sadness left her cold;
to the west, the wind howled at the season of change;
and to the south, the eagle soared through her to play.

where could she bend?
how far into the gusts
before she got eaten by a forging bear?

I understood that everything that was manifesting, false or real feelings,
psychic or unexplained connections and all they brought up, were mirrors

of something to see or understand; that the world works in mysterious ways. This form of attention appeared at the time that it did. I was grateful to 1) be brought back to life like that again, and to 2) be reminded I still had something others could see and be attracted to. Because I was convinced that the womanly seductress part of me had vanished.

I would never have an affair. But I understand why people do: to resuscitate a perished pulse. Recklessness could ignite the fire of life. It wouldn't repair feelings of identity loss, helplessness, or invisibility. It was representational. I believe illusions are meant to show something. Share something. Unearth something. I was more curious about what that was while I basked in the attention of a hot-looking Native American artist dude. *Fuckin' A*, being so wanted when you feel like a frumpy, middle-aged, menopausal woman is like a needle-delivered opioid for an identity-starved junkie.

I was glad to be on my way to Costa Rica to sort out my life. I had much bigger salmon to smoke. I wanted distance from the weird transference dance with the bear and to get to the heart of the real matter. The matter of Me.

(It) Matters of the Heart

I'd signed up for the October Soul Magic retreat in Costa Rica after attending the Lee Harris three-day workshop. Those three days were powerful and had opened up crucial new insights—particularly about the role of judgment in my life—which enabled the next steps in my discovery Flight.

Seven months had passed since the Portland workshop as I was getting ready for the Costa Rica retreat. I had many questions about where I'd been emotionally, where I was going professionally, and what I was going to do about my marriage. It's safe to say I'd been flapping tired wings for so long that feeling disoriented had become the norm. Yet, simultaneously, I had whispers assuring me that I was searching for something deeper and to keep going.

A few weeks before Soul Magic, I'd gone on a morning hike with my friend Becki. We talked a bit about my upcoming trip to Costa Rica and what I thought I was searching for. She's a skeptic about matters of self-searching in that she lives her life as pragmatically as one can. I'd describe her as a social scientist, though not in the literal sense. She believes in data. She's fascinated by the psychological process people go through in making decisions. She is curious and skeptical about all forms of research.

I love her intelligence and capacity to question things for the sake of deeper knowledge. I joke with her and call her Spock. She's one of the smartest people I know and also one of the most generous. I've come to rely on her counsel in many matters. Sometimes in our conversations, I'm reserved about my Flight—because really, if I had to put it in a category, I'd say the core of my quest is spiritual—and I don't want her to look down on me. Not that she would; that's my own projection.

She doesn't dismiss spirituality, but as a devout atheist, God, the unseen, and enlightenment aren't high on her list. However, I had shared bits of my Flight with her. On the hike, she asked me, "How will you know you've reached some milestone for what you've been searching for?" That's a fair question and in fact one I'd asked myself. How *would* I know?

Throughout the Flight, I questioned my own sanity and search. What *was* I looking for? Had I become addicted to discontentment? Was I ever going to be satisfied? Was I holding onto an illusion of what I thought life was supposed to be? It's confusing to know you're looking for something, not exactly sure what, driven to keep going, mired in doubt, and yet, unable to do anything differently.

I feebly told her I wasn't sure what the answer was. But I had a feeling I would know what I knew when I knew it.

Prior to the retreat, I kept the Costa Rica trip on the social media down-low. I think that words like "soul" and "magic" have connotations. It's easy to have opinions about concepts that seem airy-fairy. *Soul, spirit, enlightenment, love, angels, guides, expansion, consciousness, clearing, healing, transformation, energy, sacred, karma* . . . these are words I have been familiar with over the years. Yet I had judgments about what I thought the words meant. Or what they implied. Or about the people that used these words.

I'd say the spiritual realm was a step beyond my comfort zone, which followed the emotional realm, and which was equally mysterious and intermittently understood. I'd read books that most people read as spiritual bystanders, such as *The Secret* or *The Celestine Prophecy*. I'd even skimmed *The Four Agreements*. But my mind could never believe. There was only skepticism.

Even though I've had too many psychic readings to count over the past 25 years, if I *didn't* believe in something like energy or truth or things I couldn't rationally explain, why did I keep coming back to this world?

I've had readings with mediums who spoke to my dead father, grandfather, and grandmother, who provided intimate messages related to who they were in life that could not have come from an internet search. I've had dreams in which dead family members appeared that were more than just sleepytime narratives. I'd wake up with the *feeling* that they'd been present.

Aside from those who hold faith in God through traditional religion, most want to believe in something more, greater, or bigger. But this reconciliation between what a mind can *know*, what a heart *feels*, and what a soul *believes*, well, this is tricky terrain.

Whatever religion one may embrace, or perhaps just a kinship with the unseen, people that trust and feel and know and believe have my admiration. This Flight toward my Self is about the unseen.

"Who am I?" is the age-old question philosophers, sages, mystics, and scholars have pondered for thousands of years. Essentially I was asking this question, but with the added phrase " . . . without what I do?" How do I learn how to "see" my Self once I subtract the stuff and activity and expectation and busywork and title and persona and all I project?

This is the Eye I refer to. This has been what the past several years have been about. This is what drove me, almost involuntarily, toward something—toward Me.

It's hard to label the nature of this Flight. Is the search for Self only spiritual? Looking for something that's unseen could easily slip it into the spiritual category. I've got nothing better.

Violet. (the day before leaving for Costa Rica)

I'm running last minute errands the day before leaving for Costa Rica. Without any particular trigger, intense emotions begin to surface. I stop between errands and packing and go to visit my daughter at her job at Starbucks. As I watch her, green apron on, helping customers, my heart unravels. I'm flooded by how immensely proud of her I am. How much I love her. How amazing she is in so many ways. I sit in the corner, overtaken by an unencumbered heart, a side of coffee and tears flow. It's time to leave Starbucks because I don't want to be the crazy crying lady clutching a venti. I step outside and watch the breeze cradle orange leaves, twirling, gliding, as they depart familiar limbs. I inhale an essence of all that is and all that may be. A surprise angel agrees.

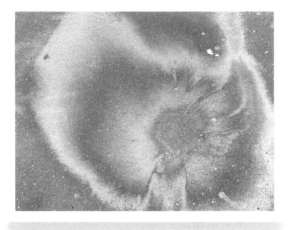

Jungle Love

Costa Rica wasn't on my radar to visit. I had no idea what to expect. I had no details about where it was on a map, the cultural environment it was known for, or the topography. But as I soon came to discover, Costa Rica, as a place, was enchanting.

The Lee Harris Soul Magic retreat was held at Blue Spirit, a large property on the Pacific coast, in an area called Nosara. The journey there began at 2:30 a.m. on Saturday. I headed to the Portland airport after a restless three hours of sleep to catch a 5 a.m. flight. From Portland to Los Angeles, then Los Angles direct to Liberia, Costa Rica. The flight was turbulent. Lots of heart-jarring shakes and rumbles along the way.

We arrived in Liberia at 3:30 in the afternoon, local time. There were 10 of us who had flown in from various places and had landed around the same time. I stepped outside of the airport into a wall of heat. A small van greeted us, still strangers, unaware of the adventure ahead. We crammed in tightly. It was a 2.5-hour drive to Blue Spirit.

Since Costa Rica is just north of the equator, it gets dark around 5 p.m. The ride to Blue Spirit was as turbulent as the flight. In addition to being afraid to fly, I also get car queasy. By the last third of the long drive, I was toast. It was dark, and I was crawling on no sleep and an empty stomach as we traversed a twisty gravel road littered with potholes. I tried to make conversation to pass time, but the rough road never ended.

I don't think I've ever been so happy to arrive somewhere. My nauseated, needing-to-pee, worn-out self spilled out into the unknown night. There were only 30 minutes until the first retreat session began, which was barely enough time to check in, get to my room, take a quick shower, brush my teeth, grab a quick bite, and rally my senses.

The main gathering hall was set up in a big semicircle. There were windows everywhere, but it was dark and I had no idea what was outside. There were 45 participants who'd come from all over the world. Slowly, people filled the seats. I could sense how spent everyone else was. The energy in the air was strange—a concoction of trepidation, anticipation, and uncertainty around what we'd all come searching for.

Lee came in at 8 p.m. He sat in the middle of the semicircle. His familiar voice was a comfort. Just as he began to share what the coming week would be about, huge flashes of lightening lit up the room. Thunder rumbled the windows. The electricity outside seemed to want its way into the room.

We were given a microphone to pass around, briefly introducing ourselves and saying where we were from. Just as the first person was about to speak, a giant hawk flew into the room, crashed into a window, and knocked itself out. We were all stunned when we realized what had occurred.

As serendipity would have it, the hawk crash-landed right next to a guy who happened to study birds. He leapt into action and knew exactly what to do for the stunned hawk to protect it, without getting injured himself by the bird's sharp beak and talons. He carefully cradled the stunned hawk and carried it to an open window where it could gather its senses and safely fly away. Meanwhile, lightening was flashing like fireworks.

We resumed introducing ourselves, and these were my first connections with a highly engaging group of interesting, dynamic individuals. After the opening ceremony concluded with a musical healing, I went downstairs to my room, beyond exhausted. But the strangeness wasn't over yet. In my room was a glass door leading to a balcony. When I looked over, I saw this:

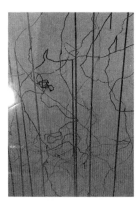

The condensation on the window had created a funky pattern, the likes of which I'd never seen. What was strange was that the pattern reflected exactly how I felt inside. It also mirrored the crazy energy of the lightening and the hawk incident—scrambled, disjointed, chaotic. The pattern was fascinating.

(same window, the next morning)

Even more bizarre, each night thereafter, the window showed something new. The variables of weather hadn't changed. Each night's control factors were similar. I documented what transpired. Here (in order) is what the window looked like each night at the same time of the night:

Some have seen Jesus in toast or Mother Mary in clouds. Perhaps there's some scientific explanation for the condensation patterns, but whatever it was or wasn't, they felt like a manifestation of what I was feeling, as if to remind me about trusting the unexplained. I'd spent 51 years using my mind to fabricate beliefs and reality. Sometimes the magic, the unexplained, like a hummingbird, provides comfort about synchronicity.

A majority of us have lost all sense of wonder. Synchronicities happen all the time, but we're too mind-focused to see them. I took in the awe of seeing what the window showed each night. I asked around, and no one on my floor had a window that had done what mine had.

* * * * *

Before the retreat, when I was asked who Lee Harris was, I stumbled over how to respond. When embarking on spiritual endeavors, it's easy to trip over words or descriptions to others to explain the what or who or how of such pursuits. Lee's website says he is a "globally acclaimed intuitive messenger, transformational leader, musician & artist." It's true, he is these things.

If you're on your Flight, you'll find physical circumstances that help bring your Self forward more clearly. It took years, but I listened to the whispers and followed the crumbs and they delivered me to the places, people, events, and circumstances that helped Me "see" my Self. There are lots of teachers, healers, counselors, workshops, books, and videos that offer an array of healing information. That's what I was seeking; an ultimate healing for a broken, forgotten, out-of-shape, ignored, shy, vulnerable, tender, delicate, skeptical, cautious, and hopeful heart. Read, watch, listen, question, and explore anyone or any teachings that you feel resonate.

The first morning of the retreat, Sunday, I took an early walk down to the beach to survey where I was, since I'd arrived in the dark. Behind the lodge at Blue Spirit was a vast, canopied valley and hillsides blanketed by trees. Howler monkeys growled from the treetops in unison. I'd never heard such a sound before!

I strolled downhill along a gravel path toward the ocean. It was lush with flowers and towering palms. When I reached the ocean, the tide was out. Playa Guiones is the crescent strip of beach where Blue Spirit is located, in the area of Nosara. It stretches for miles. Amazing speckled and creamy seashells dotted the sand. It was only 6:30 a.m., yet it was warm and humid. I peered out over the Pacific Ocean and felt far away from home. I thought about how much Mark would love the scenery.

The initial workshop began at 10:30 a.m. Lee spoke about the week's intentional agenda—meaning the framework for the energy work he would guide us through. We were given two different colored pieces of paper. One was to write down what we wanted to *release* from our lives, the other was to proclaim the *intentions* for our lives. There were two shiny gold bowls in the middle of the room placed upon a beautiful, round, purple and magenta blanket. We were given a few minutes to jot our thoughts down. Each person placed their papers in the respective bowls. I can't even remember what I wrote.

Workshop sessions consisted of a mixture of teaching, discussion, and hearing people's stories about where they were in their lives, sharing experiences, and intuitive readings that Lee gave. Lee would focus on one person's story, but it was easy to see something relevant in nearly everyone's stories.

The week also included a few excursions. One was a gorgeous guided hike to a waterfall called Mala Noche. This was a stunning adventure to a large watering hole fed by a rushing waterfall. The water was surprisingly warm and it was fun to see how everyone responded to the sense of freedom and beauty. I sat beneath the waterfall on a slippery rock. It was incredible to have the rushing water pounding over my head and onto my skin and to hear how a waterfall sounds.

One of the other retreat excursions was ziplining, which I had zero desire to do. Those who stayed behind were offered an afternoon of painting. Outside on the veranda of the main dining area, tables were set up with tubes of colorful paint, brushes, small canvases, markers, and stencils. There was a brief demonstration utilizing the materials, to jumpstart creative possibilities for anyone intimidated by paint.

I sat at a table and initially observed how each person was going about painting. A psychoanalyst would have had a field day!

Typically I'd have had all kinds of judgment about what I was doing, how good it looked, what the art was *supposed* to be. Yet I stayed with the paint. I chose not to use a brush. I placed bright pink, yellow, turquoise, and red paint onto a paper palette. I stuck my index and middle finger into the cold pigment. Admiring the rich colors of my fingertips I connected them to the paper and slowly moved them around. For the next 40 minutes, I got lost in the land of color. There was something primal about rolling fingers doused in pigments across a canvas.

* * * * *

During a workshop session midway through the week, I had a breakthrough about my situation with Mark. The topic was recognizing one's boundaries, and the focus was on love relationships. Fortunately with Mark, crossing or enforcing them isn't an issue. Lee mentioned a statement that struck me: Does the person in your life **support**, **protect**, **respect** and **love** your individual power?

That gave me something to ponder. I could say that over the nine years we'd been together, Mark had done all of these. He had given me plenty of room to roam.

During challenging times in my marriage and throughout my Dark Flight, a question had plagued me that I'd been asked by several friends: "If there were so many differences between you and Mark, what did you initially fall in love with?" I couldn't answer. I couldn't see where we were and where we'd been as individuals or as a couple. Thoughts and feelings and points of relationship reference had become muddy.

I tried to imagine who I was at the time I'd gotten together with him. Perhaps coming out of a divorce, I was needy when I met him. Or I didn't know myself well enough to know what I needed. Or I'd only recently became aware of what I needed—mostly emotionally—as I searched and discovered and formed a new way of seeing the world. Of seeing my Self. And that entailed needing new things, new conversations, new forms of interaction and intimacy. I knew I needed a higher yet deeper level of perception. We were quickly flowing down separate streams.

Between the many frustrating, dead-end conversations we'd had the past few years related to politics, my Flight, and the sad state of our marriage, I wasn't sure if Mark 1) had the desire, or 2) the capacity to go deeper. The potential answers weren't hopeful prospects. I'd told myself a lot of stories about Mark and us because nothing had shifted and we were getting more distant by the day.

Before going to Costa Rica, my mind had crafted three conclusion scenarios. With each scenario, unanswerable questions swirled about what marriage is meant to be.

The first scenario was that we would live together as strangers, leading separate lives, but for the sake of financial and logistical convenience, we'd continue as we'd been. I'd have to become independent and sexless, and we would be like many married couples: in quiet desperation for the sake of the status quo.

The second scenario was to part ways. Although I didn't want to imagine this as a possibility, it was a possibility. I visualized the For Sale sign on the house, purging assets, the conversation with my kids, search for a new apartment, damage control on Facebook, waking up alone, being single, building a life of quiet-yet-satisfied solitude in the sunset of my life with cats, books, friends, and travel.

The third scenario was to drudge through counseling, come up against the same maybe unsolvable issues, and try to place a ton of plugs in a leaky ship. There were no envisioned outcomes with this path, per se, but having the option in the mix temporarily avoided the other two. This assumption was based on stories I'd constructed about Mark in order to make sense of and find answers for what had become a painful stalemate. I had been afraid to grow for fear of leaving him behind.

As I sat in a chair listening to Lee's words echo, and realized that Mark had *supported, protected, respected,* and *loved* my power, I remembered what I had fallen in love with. It was *the person I saw in him.* When we first met, I was able to *see* Mark clearly in ways he was unable to see himself. I'd seen his person, his heart, if you will. And over the years, especially in the past few, there had been major disconnects in the person I'd initially seen and the person whose words had shown up in the world.

This disparity between heart and words can be true for any of us, but eventually I didn't know which to believe—the heart I'd initially seen or his words (particularly around the political realm). I only saw reactions (to me, to conflict) and from these, I created stories to help dictate what to "do." They weren't, however, helpful for how to "see."

The revelatory dots connected. Sitting in the semicircle, in a beautifully vast room of a lodge on a Costa Rican hill, surrounded by windows peering out to the ocean below, an entirely other paradigm of marriage began to crystalize.

I'd initially seen a compassion or rather a softness in Mark. Given that, I could extend an invitation to him—to dig a little deeper. Not because it was an ultimatum; I wasn't asking him to be something or someone he wasn't. Given my own growth trajectory, having someone on their own heart-centric path felt reasonable. I understood it would be different than mine. If he was unwilling or chose not to explore the idea, then at least I'd know the dialog was more honest than the stories I'd been telling myself. I could come to the relationship from love about what I needed, instead of from judgment and criticism.

* * * * *

It was easy to slip into a rhythm of the heart during the week in Costa Rica. It was so tropical and untamed. Crazy, unexplained magical things occurred every day, occurrences a mind couldn't explain. Oversized critters with big wings and big eyes showed up at odd moments to affirm a particular discovery; fireflies popped in and out of total darkness like intermittent sparks of comfort as I stood by the ocean one night and cried beneath a canopy of palm fronds. It was as if a dream was being lived inside the dream and I could no longer tell where one life dream ended and the heart dream began.

One such event involved receiving insight from someone or something other than me, even though I was the one writing it down. The exercise is called channeled writing. The idea is that you sit in silence with a pen and paper and just write what comes. No thoughts about what's appearing but you keep in the flow of what's pouring out.

Over my years of spiritual dabbling, I'd done this exercise before. And honestly, it was one that annoyed me. I'd be writing and I'd be thinking about writing and I'd be thinking that I was thinking about writing and words would stiffly come out and I was certain my mind was telling me what to write and before the damn exercise was done I'd call bullshit on the whole thing.

You know what channeled writing reminded me of? Remember playing *Ouija* and you and your friend had fingers on the plastic heart and it would slowly move across the board and you'd each swear neither of you was moving it but one or both of you was moving it? Yeah, like that. Channeled writing was the bullshit, you-know-that-I-know-that-you-know version of the *Ouija* board. Until it wasn't.

We were asked to take out our books and start writing. And without thought or hesitation, words spilled out on the paper. Only they were coming from my hand and definitely not my head. This time there was something different. The entire experience was different. Words were clear, unfettered, and broadcast from a place with which I was not familiar.

They were not my words. My mind distinctly knew it wasn't the source. I wasn't even cognizant about what was being written down. The words kept coming, I kept writing, and when they were done, they were done. I sat back looking at a filled page covered with words, bewildered by what had transpired.

It was sort of cool. I was in on something unexplainable! I felt grown up. Like I'd gotten the secret handshake. I wasn't sure what to do with the discovery, where to put it, but I knew I didn't want to start explaining it away. I knew what I had *felt*. I was clear on the differences between past experiences and this one. I decided one thing I could do (since the words had come out so fast) was to go back and read what the hell had been written! When I got done reading, I was in awe of the writing and its message:

> What does your heart have to teach?
> What does your heart offer for you?
> What has the moment of being kept open in places
> of uncertainty?
> How will the moment create the moments of others?
> Does awakening need to have to process an unshielding?
> Does it create a more fertile playground to laugh, to love, to
> give, to create,
> to showcase an essence of life we rarely see?
> Does an unshielding leave you open or really, just alive?
> Will an unshielding happen in faith, or, in motion?
> How will you know?
> you will know.
> You will understand the difference in how you free your senses
> into what's around you.
> It will feel strange, but magical and complete.
> Fire fire fire
> fire fire fire
> fire up fire out
> fire in fire doubt.

I'd never use that word "unshielding." This word would never be in my vernacular. Yet it was a good word to describe the Flight and the process I'd undertaken. I had protected my heart with my head for my entire life. Yet I read the words. I sat in my chair feeling fluttery.

* * * * *

The magical Costa Rican Soul Train kept rollin'. (If I was reading this book, I may have called bullshit by now . . . LOL) The next day we had a few hours of free time before the afternoon session. I grabbed a towel at the front desk and went down to the sparkling infinity pool. It's surrounded by gorgeous green tropical foliage. I draped the towel over one of the lounge chairs and plopped down. Aside from hearing monkeys growl from distant canopies, the only sounds were of trickling water and a slight breeze rustling palm leaves. I was alone and it was nice.

As I settled in the lounger, I closed my eyes. I inhaled warm fresh air through my nose down into the tubes of my lungs. I drifted off, feeling grateful that after I'd been on the Flight for so long, my heart was starting to feel clearer and more at peace. Then my mind chimed in, "How do you know if any of this is real?"

Annoyed, I opened my eyes and sat up. The sudden light was searing. As if on cue, I glanced over to a barely visible patch of tiny red flowers nestled within a circular planter of green foliage and there it was—a brilliant blue hummingbird, just a few feet in front of me. As much as I had been looking forward to seeing hummingbirds in Costa Rica, I hadn't seen a single one the whole time I'd been there. (And wouldn't see another for the remainder of the trip.) The blue was incredible, almost like a sapphire. The hummingbird floated in front of me and the flowers for a quick second, and then disappeared.

* * * * *

Internal changes along my Flight over several years were slow and incremental. Some were remarkable, while others were barely traceable. I can't pinpoint exact moments when my wings headed in a different direction. But somehow, affirming moments kept showing up.

Day Five something monumental occurred. In a whisper of a moment I at last greeted my Self from the other side.

Going to the Santa Fe casita had been intended to metaphorically stick my hand out, as a gesture, to introduce myself to my Self. Like, "Hi, I'm showing up, here to meet you, whenever you're ready." I visualized the me I'd always known—the thinking, doing, being version of me, the hologram version who had survived on a steady life diet of thoughts and productivity—actually stretching out my hand to an empty space I couldn't see but trusted was there.

The empty space had been what I'd imagined, felt, and couldn't describe. It was all I'd been looking for. The empty space I reached out to was Me. *The* Me. I suppose the sensation might be compared to an adopted child who wants to know who their parents are, spends years imagining who they might be, and how that missing puzzle piece conveys something to complete who they are. It's more about nurturing the yearning and not necessarily what's to be discovered.

How can we rely on something we feel, in our heart, through our heart, or from our heart, that is not quantifiable, doesn't produce anything, has no real definition and doesn't derive from what we comprehend as reality?

I want anyone who reads this to know that I honestly don't believe real moments of connection to our Selves are necessarily about magical instances of the unexplained. It's possible they may happen, but it's entirely more probable they won't. It doesn't make your Flight any less real or substantial. The whole immersion of midlife identity, of spirit, of Self, and of belonging doesn't require fancy retreats, spiritual gurus, travel, or external sources providing answers. If you're in it, fuck it, just be where and how and who you are—that's more than enough. You're doing your best, just keep *flying*.

The nature of this Flight toward Self, a new identity, a more soul-full emergence of who we are, minus everything we construct from our minds, requires the utter dismantling of most things we believed about who we are. We can't "know" what a heart feels like, sounds like, or looks like if we've never traversed that realm before.

It's impossible to "know" in your mind who you are from a heart that is what ultimately comprises you. The lack of reconciliation between these two is the pain. This is grief. This is the disconnection. This is the discontentment of an unsolvable problem. This is the crash between the identity you with which you have a cognitive relationship and the identity of your heart, your Self that's whispering to be known, be seen, be felt and discovered.

This is the Flight.

The Flight delivers you to landmarks within yourself and your mind that shine a spotlight on what's keeping you held together and offers checkpoints to break down barriers that keep you trapped.

Recognizing there was another Self—*the* Self—was a checkpoint. Recognizing (through force of traumatic circumstances) that my perception of my identity wasn't in fact my only identity, was a checkpoint. Taking photos of hummingbirds were small but significant checkpoints. Recognizing Judgment as a tremendous beast that prevented me from connecting with my heart (for a myriad of reasons) was a checkpoint. Recognizing that expectations ran the show of how I was being in the world was a checkpoint. Recognizing I was afraid of a more tender Me, a more fragile Me, a more unknown Me that was there, had always been there, but had been left behind, was a checkpoint. Setting up an environment (Santa Fe) to have a conversation with my Self, as my Grand

Gesture, for the sole sake of being with discomfort, to extend my hand as an invitation was a major checkpoint.

And there *I* was. Sitting in a gorgeous hall, the extraordinary moment had just slipped in. My Self had grasped the extended hand. I felt it. I clutched the hand that had been hanging in wait and said, "Welcome." I greeted Me. That feeling, that longing, to find my Self— yeah, I connected with her. I pondered how long I'd been Flying. Yet I knew there was more.

I felt relief, and uncertainty, and trepidation, but I also felt whole and clear and, for a moment, elusive peace. Unification. The me I'd always "known" and the Self from my heart who was waiting to become *known*, connected. It was a surreal feeling. My heart received a tug and pulsated with inpouring emotion. I got that the moment was fleeting and probably not going to appear again for some time. But for that moment I was on the In side.

Ecstatic Dance – Part Do
(As in Do-Over)

Night Five meant No Panic at the Blue Spirit Disco ecstatic dance head-quarters. This aspect of physical expression was on the agenda, as I suspected it would be. Ahhh yes, old friend, we meet again—only this time, I had some moves.

As the requests for no talking and to take breaks outside were explained, I surveyed the room. I sensed some were familiar with the exercise, but I was curious about those who weren't. When I'd been in their shoes, I wasn't sure what to make of it all until the music started. That was when panic set in.

In Costa Rica, in the spirit of magic, I was excited for the dance to begin. It had been eight months since the Portland ecstatic dance—a pivotal Flight checkpoint for me. It had clearly revealed Judgment and shifted my understanding about one aspect that was keeping me from Me.

The music started. The room was vast with plenty of dance space to spare. People twirled in the humid night air, alone, together, shifting and shaking to the beats. I was in the middle of the room, moving freely, taking in all the rich happiness around me. I could see how far I'd come in eight months. It was remarkable to make allowance for my heart's progress.

I loved that moment. Reeling in the connection with amazingly brave people I'd grown to know; the freedom permeating the room; the simple fun of dancing without judgment; and a sense of accomplishment for how far I'd come. If I could have taken one snapshot that represented the Costa Rica experience, it would have been of this scene.

The familiar ecstatic dance playlist kicked in. Chaka Khan's "Ain't Nobody" came on. Yep, Chaka, we're reunited and now it's Me that's floating like the butterfly. A beautifully blue, gracefully free South American butterfly.

Time for Me to Fly

By the end of the week in Costa Rica, I was floating on a cosmic cloud. I'd bonded with many wonderful people, insights into things I'd struggled with had crystallized, and I was on my way toward optimism I'd not had for years. Not to mention the unexplained magic stuff. The last night's ceremony would seal the deal on a beautiful adventure.

In the late afternoon, we gathered in the hall upstairs for a final session. Reflections and observations from the week were shared. The bittersweet sentiment of saying goodbye to our cocooned world of love and friendship reminded me of a last night at summer camp. We'd grown together in that week. We'd seen each other blossom in the midst of a crazy matrix of jungle luck and energetic fortune.

In the middle of the room, on the blanket, were stones; clear and rose quartz. At the close of the session, each person picked out one of each. We walked to the beach in collective silence for sunset.

I shuffled down the path I'd walked many times that week. Together we walked, accompanied by crunching gravel. Once at the beach we scattered. The tide was out. The water twinkled as gentle waves rolled in. Wispy clouds glowed from the blood-orange sun dangled above the blue horizon. I walked into the water just below my knees and tucked my feet beneath the warm ocean blanket. I faced the sun to take in the light.

The breeze whispered heat as I embraced the week's culmination. I was silent, yet everything crackled with life. The band above the horizon deepened to a pumpkin color as we watched the sun slip down. Feathery clouds were lit by shiny beams until soft pink settled in. I tossed my stones into the ocean.

The experience had been an incubation: a time and place where the alchemy of the unseen and unexplained, plus love and community and compassion and energy forged together.

* * * * *

As we wind down, keep in mind that this is *a* story. It is *one* story. I've offered tidbits. These are pieces of my puzzle but not absolutes for anyone else. I don't think sequestering oneself, faraway retreats, or following any one path or any one person is the answer. Much of what transpired for me over several years took place in private, so much so that I was in it but most of the time not even aware of how events were unfolding. The questions I had related to Self-discovery were more feelings about things I didn't understand.

A Dark Flight of the Self is incredibly lonely. An identity is delicate and stubborn, idealized and impractical, honest and untruthful, contradictory and absolute, ever-changing and permanent.

While I glided for years within a question that had no answers, I subsequently *flew* into places of darkness that were unkind to my Self, creating images of unattainable backdrops and designing unforgiving odds. I realize this now. My heart breaks for the tired spirit who was doing her best, yet was entirely lost.

We're living in strange times. Political division clogs unified possibility. Social media and the projection of false personas supersede the raw nature of life's experiences—they keep us mired in fog and distant from authentic connections that never have a chance to blossom. Hearts are stuffed away and suffocated by expectation, judgment, and the elusive lie of productivity.

We're starved for true connection, drowned out by noise, thirsty to be seen, and afraid hope may betray us. Yet, we show up. And that counts for everything. Listen closely to your whispers and keep your eyes peeled for the crumbs. They know something you don't yet.

You're not alone. Many of us are lost, worn-down little birds flying through hostile, lonely skies. From time to time, we comingle with other lost birds at various cloud stops along our Flights. We're in grief over the people we thought we'd become; grief over the people we thought we were; and in grief that midlife has left us searching to find a way home. We're imperfect, confused, wonderfully fragile, and amazing. Our hearts are powerful, resilient, magical forces that patiently await our eventual landings.

All my lonely experiences coalesced in lost pieces that I collected like talismen from various checkpoints. I may have been Flying, but my heart never left. I couldn't have seen my Self until whatever barriers that kept Me hidden had been dismantled. Those barriers protected the total structure of an identity that necessarily crumbled. Painful, indeed. Required, for sure.

Like any magical adventure, the dream was nearing an end—but not without one final enchanted crescendo. Most of us were departing Blue Spirit on Saturday morning, catching various shuttles to the Liberia airport based on flight times. The hotel lobby was a hub of people waiting for shuttles, saying goodbyes, hugging, crying, laughing, and again, through the texture of emotion in the air, I was transported to the final shalom circle at my Jewish summer camp. Together, we'd become something.

Group by group, people departed over the next hour as each shuttle departed. The din of the lobby grew quieter. My group was called for departure at 11 a.m. Several of the same women had been with me on the dark, bumpy shuttle on the way to Blue Spirit when we'd first arrived. That felt like an eternity ago.

I was happily surprised to see a large, newer van parked below for the airport trek. Better still, the air conditioning was cranked when I got inside. As I sat looking out the window, waiting for the last few people to board, I was lost in thought. My mind kicked in by doing its busybee thing to unravel my Self from the moment. I wanted to be ahead of the discomfort.

When all were on board, the van rolled down the hillside toward the main road. I was thinking of the airport. Thinking of my bed. Trying to imagine real life at home—to visualize tangible surroundings in order to try on what my new life would feel like in an old setting.

By the time we'd crossed the Blue Spirit gate and reached the main road, my mind had focused on the airport. That was when Corrine, one of the retreat attendees, realized out loud that she'd left something behind. Several women sitting by her chimed in for the van to stop.

Fuck! I thought to myself as the van came to a halt. And a sincere *Double fuck!* when I discovered that what she had left behind wasn't a laptop or a camera, but a stuffed animal. Impatience swelled, judgment sneered, and I marveled at how quickly feelings of compassion and sister-hood had disappeared. Not even 10 minutes in the outside world and I'm all *Namaste, bitches!*

Everyone else on the bus was supportive. They reassured her. Looking at the bus clock, I tried to reason. *Obviously it meant something to her.* Corrine stepped out of the shuttle and walked toward the guard gate to phone the lodge's front desk and let them know what she'd forgotten.

To avoid a pissy fit, I whipped out my phone. I wondered if we had wi-fi because we were still on property grounds. I got onto Facebook to check. We did. I scrolled down a little, and a little more, and the next scroll was so shocking, so unimaginable, it siphoned my breath. I couldn't believe what I was seeing. (Keep in mind that Facebook algorithms are entirely random regarding what's seen at any given moment. Pop on five minutes before or five minutes after any pinpoint in time, and you'll get a completely different scroll.)

On the screen was the image of a cover from *Local Living* maga-zine. It was old—from five years earlier. It had been posted by someone I didn't know and wasn't even Facebook friends with. It was the cover that accompanied a fun story I'd written about a group of local rocker dudes who were dads. She had posted the *Local Living* cover, with the caption, "Still looking good and rocking after all these years!!"

Because we'd stopped in that five minutes, I'd gone on Facebook. If Corinne hadn't forgotten, then remembered she'd forgotten her stuffed animal, if we hadn't stopped, I wouldn't have gone on Facebook and I wouldn't have seen this neon light of a gift and message that said, *How fucking strange and unexplainable and perfectly suited is this? A journey ends exactly from where it began.*

The magazine cover was from the time I was flying high in my public persona, beneath the wings of a veneered identity. A place and me I didn't even recognize now. The cover was like a launched rocket in space reminding me how the Dark Flight had been ignited. Chances of seeing it were one in a million. It was a message only I would hear. Sure, there can be math and logic to explain it. But really?

The golf cart carrying Corrine's precious cargo arrived at the van. I still couldn't fully absorb the incredible message meant for me. Li'l ol' Me—a Me that was finally being seen, and experiencing grace and magic and love and a heart bursting full of things. It was amazing.

As we pulled away, clarity snapped like a spark. I had nothing to do with that moment, and everything to do with that moment. Lessons about patience were profound. In my mind, I'd been ready to go. Ready to separate. *But I wasn't done just yet.* I stared out the window and watched the rolling green hills, big puffy clouds, and palm trees sway above grassy fields. I had needed just five more minutes. Five more minutes for the possible to be unveiled.

Something else needed to be learned.

Something more needed to be seen.

Something true needed to be reminded.

Something buried deep within my heart needed to be felt.

I needed to be brought back to the moment from where I came. I needed to be shown where my Dark Flight of the Self had begun. And with that, in a single spark, I'd landed.

I really had landed.

Blame the First Ending
on Sitcoms
(or)
Blinders of Idealism

(Between the last chapter you just read, and here, I invoke a loud SCREECH sound of a needle dragged across a vinyl record to disrupt your regularly scheduled tidy ending...!)

The last words of that last chapter would have been a nice ending, wouldn't they? Well, I'm not trying to upset happily-ever-after Hollywood here, but after all we've been through, I think you deserve the brief but necessary truth of what really happened next.

Several months after I got home from Costa Rica, a few key events messed with my perfect landing. Similar to the northern lights not being as advertised, neither was the grand finale in my identity search. The first disruptor was a knock in the noggin that debunked the charade of idealism.

Idealism is defined as: the practice of forming or pursuing ideals, especially unrealistically. The *idealism* of youth. synonyms: utopianism, wishful thinking, romanticism, fantasizing, quixotism, daydreaming, impracticability.

As a child, I was heavily influenced by 1970s sitcom television—at the end of 22 minutes, all misunderstandings, calamities, and touchy situations came together as sweetly as corn syrup: Mr. Kotter, an underpaid high school teacher, capped off challenging days with troubled students (known as the *Sweathogs*) over dinner with his understanding wife, Julie, in their tiny apartment, and by sharing a funny parable about his uncle; Janet, Jack, and Chrissie were in perpetual roommate turmoil over how to pay rent or fix botched lies hiding the truth from Mr. Roper about Jack's non-homosexuality, then patched up disagreements over beers at the Regal Beagle; Even the unflappable Fonz made the impossible seem possible by making a broken jukebox instantly play with the pound of a fist.

Candy-coated solutions were engrained. Not that I believed nicely bow-tied resolutions to complicated conflicts were how life worked, but that was the way they were depicted. I suppose I so badly wanted those resolutions for myself, too, when it came to answers for the big internal questions I had.

When I got back from Costa Rica in November, I was floating on a self-help cloud. While there, I'd had many unexplained moments of synchronicity and substantial discoveries about myself and my marriage. I felt a sense of belonging. Things with Mark were on a solid road to repair.

Although there were people at Blue Spirit from all over the world, the group had included seven people from Portland, including me. We connected as a smaller group within the larger group. When we got home from the amazing experience, our smaller group had those specific memories. Our interactions had become a strong common bond. The people within this group were like me; they'd been searching and were open about deep fears and hopes. I felt an immediate kinship and comfort with them.

In the group were six women and one man, a son of one of the women. We saw each other on a semi-regular basis back in Portland. We had gatherings at people's homes, we sang karaoke one night, and we even spent a weekend together at the Oregon coast in a beautiful house I procured. Two others from the Costa Rica adventure came up from Southern California for the beach weekend.

What I appreciated was that this group stayed connected. We could talk about feelings or things we were going through in ways that weren't readily available in daily life. There was a realness about fears and an understood language around desires for a more open heart. Sometimes conversations would be free-flowing and sometimes they wanted to watch a Lee video or do a Lee-centric activity as a group. Although I was impartial, there were times when these seemed a little narrow.

We'd planned a Memorial Day weekend gathering in Huntington Beach at one of the women's houses. There were 10 of us in total (six from

Portland, two from Southern California, and one woman even came from New Jersey). The house was lovely. It had a beautiful yard complete with a pool and hot tub, there was enough room to accommodate us all, and our hostess was very gracious.

Initially, I'd been trepidatious about going. It was an expense I couldn't really afford and the timing wasn't great. My nephew was graduating from college two weeks later and I'd be back down to Southern California.

But I went, the weekend was fun, and I was glad I'd gone. It was a mixture of deep talk (intermittent one-on-ones as well as group discussions), delicious food, sightseeing, fun evenings around the fire pit drinking tasty adult beverages, sharing stories and laughter.

A highlight of my weekend was taking Saturday morning to visit my older brother Len, who had moved to Long Beach the year before. I'd not yet had the chance to see his new place, and given that Long Beach was only a 20-minute drive, I seized the opportunity. My brother's new place was nice. Right in the heart of downtown, which is experiencing a development surge. We had lunch, got caught up, walked to the marina. It was a rare treat to spend one-on-one time with my brother. What with kids and spouses, this was something we'd not done in years.

After sharing a meaningful visit, I drove back to Huntington Beach. The group had gone to Laguna for the day to sightsee. I hung at the house and enjoyed solitary time until they came back later that night. The remainder of the evening involved more alcohol and stories around the firepit. I thought that since we were together, it would be nice to convey some of what I'd written about our Costa Rica experience—to evoke shared memories.

I began to read my recollections. After a page or so, I looked around the circle to gauge the response. I was self-conscious; after all, this was my creative effort. But there was a lack of favorable response; my thoughts weren't stirring up what I'd hoped. I guess I'd had a vision of the old days, when people shared stories around the fire—fostering a sense of camaraderie. I stopped reading, then laughed off the uncomfortable misfire moment. The others moved on, and soon they were topless in the hot tub dancing to Beyonce. I chose to hang by the fire with a cocktail.

The next morning was my departure. Everyone else was staying for a few more days. I said goodbyes, drove to the airport, and arrived back in Portland thinking it had been a lovely weekend of connection, conversation, and (for lack of a better term) consciousness.

* * * * *

Two weeks later, I got a phone call from Fran. She was the oldest of the group. She asked if I had a few minutes. I told her I was stepping into a doctor's appointment and that I had about five minutes.

Fran said that after careful consideration, she and the others felt that it was in their best interest if I was no longer part of the group. They deemed that my "behavior" was a hindrance to the elevation of their highest vibration; that me "dropping in and out of the group throws off the entire force field." The examples she gave were that I had left the group to go see my brother, and that I had spent time away from the group in a restaurant where we had all gone for dinner. (I had indeed spoken to a nice couple for a few minutes in the bar of the restaurant.) At one point, she suggested that I look for the lesson they were teaching me about my "behavior."

I was rendered speechless. It took a moment for the shock to wear off and to realize that I was getting kicked off the spiritual island. As Fran continued to share the reasons I was no longer group-worthy, I felt the sting of hurt and rejection. The extremely visceral feelings I had—that I was being ganged up on and shunned—reminded me of junior high, and I said as much. With no time to process or respond in a coherent way because I had to go into my doctor's appointment, I started to cry and said I had to go. The rest of the day I felt like I was 13 years old and suddenly no longer popular.

My heart hurt. This was a group I trusted. This was a sense of belonging absent from other aspects of my life. Why didn't they like me anymore? What had I really done?

The next few days I got numerous texts from Fran on behalf of "the group." Honestly, I didn't even know who comprised the group. I had suspicions of who maybe four of them were, but I wasn't sure. Our previous few get-togethers had not had the same rosters. There was one woman from Portland who had arrived in Huntington Beach after I left. Then there were the two women from Southern California and the one from New Jersey. Were they in on this, too?

Fran's drive-by texts lamented more of the same, supported all the justifications, though I did especially appreciate one zinger: "Remember, it's all about love."

I chose not to answer the texts because honestly, there was nothing to say. The paradox of their "enlightenment" through a lens of such judgment was not lost on me, and would become a catalyst for the day Idealism died.

I felt hurt for a couple of days. Was this how enlightened people treat others? Do they impose conditions for how a process should go—whether for an individual or within a group? Do they feel better about their own spiritual path when they tell others what's flawed in theirs? In fact, the hypocrisy of the whole incident turned me off from all the spiritual stuff I'd been reading, and temporarily removed any desire to be part of anything in that realm. I know many are spiritually thirsty. Sometimes words from those we believe have answers is a refreshing drink. I say sip all the liquids—just don't drown.

I get feeling lost. I enjoy being part of community. But I don't want to always be searching. I'd been looking "out there" for what's "in here" for years.

Because of judgment from the group, my eyes were suddenly propped wide open. For the first time, I could clearly see how my idealism wanted to sugar-coat unpolished edges. I also saw that a tender Self's messiness, jagged lines, and individuality cannot be framed. *That's* the lesson I learned.

I'm telling you this because a search for answers to deep questions, identity, meaning, and belonging can be extremely confusing. We are fragile in pursuit. We want to feel that we belong and that connection with others will smooth our rough edges. There's nothing wrong with wanting these things, but in some instances there's a danger of overidealizing— whether it's who we're with, what we think we've learned, or what we believe to be self-evident. In a search for Self, these misperceptions may actually work against you. If you hang your hat on a single track of discoveries or people or beliefs, you leave no room for what actually may come to be discovered as your own.

So I admit it: I overidealized the experience in Costa Rica and some of the people I met. I was swept up by the language, the words, the moment, the environment, the group influence. When it came to real world interactions, the group didn't want me part of their gang because I wasn't responding the way they would. I wasn't behaving like they were. What they perceived as my experience wasn't mirroring theirs. And I don't want that kind of prescribed, conditional "spirituality" in my life. Especially as I'm seeking clarity. We need more love. We need more understanding. People who search are extremely vulnerable.

Something I know now, at 51 years old, is that individual answers to huge questions about life and our respective places in it are an amalgamation of individual experiences. Your truth, your understanding, your sense of self coalesces when and how it coalesces. With all the weirdness of midlife transition, I certainly don't need judgment around how it's supposed to look or unfold. Nor would I ever cast stones in the direction of someone whose ways of achieving such a transition are different.

Even though we want to be liked, I accept that not everyone will like me. Fran said I should look for the lesson they were teaching me—well, what I learned was to stop idealizing. I'm not going to find my Self in the land of others.

For the record, none of what transpired on my spiritual journey in Costa Rica was bad or anything less than amazing. I'm not knocking "the group" or their path of spiritual pursuit. They can pursue it how they best see fit for themselves. What I am saying is that the lessons of *any* group may be better understood as part of individual discovery. Self-exploration continues.

The idealization of something may constrict, cloud, or even overcompensate for the reality of our lives and the knowing we hold about our lives. We can't always be so high. We need to come down. We are who we are, and we are *where* we are in our spiritual paths. These paths should be ever-evolving, ever-questioned, yet ever-allowed in all their messiness and daily uncertainty.

P.S. I've Got M.S.

Recently, I was at a conference in Vancouver, B.C. While taking an elevator ride down from the 24th floor, I struck up a conversation with a fellow rider. It was 8:30 a.m. I'd had one cup of coffee but was ass-dragging tired. As I started to speak, words came out slurred, like I'd been drinking. I was startled and embarrassed that my co-rider might think I'd pulled an all-nighter. I tried to straighten out my words, fix them mid-speech, but nothing helped. So I shut up. After that incident and throughout the day, I felt out of it. Spacey, airy, like I was floating. Maybe I was just exhausted from travel.

Slurred speech occurred to varying degrees several more times at the conference. When I got home on Friday, I told Mark what had happened. I asked him to listen to how I was speaking. He confirmed that my speech was off.

Saturday night we were set to have our friends Joan and Bob over for dinner. I'd been looking forward to seeing them, but Saturday afternoon I called Joan to request a rain check. Joan is a nurse and when I explained what was going on, she suggested I go to urgent care in case I'd had a minor stroke or my blood pressure was high. She said that if I'd had a stroke, the more time that passed after the initial incident, the harder it would be to address.

Mark took me to urgent care. There was a three-hour wait. We were surrounded by sick people and germs. All I wanted was to have my vitals checked, be assured that my blood pressure wasn't high, and go home. My left arm and hand were numb and tingling.

My name was finally called. My blood pressure was checked; it was high. The doctor performed other diagnostic tests and it was clear my left side—both my arm and leg—had pronounced weakness. He expressed his concern that I might have had a stroke and told me to go to the emergency room.

Mark drove us to the hospital. I was scared and my thoughts were jumbled. Once I was admitted, I put on the fashionable paper gown and waited until it was my turn for the MRI. I asked for sedatives to avert claustrophobia.

As I sat in the tube in a semi-induced fog, I listened to the loud machine clunking, knocking, and churning. I vacillated between keeping my eyes shut, reading the "This MRI is a happy MRI" sticker above my eyes, and clutching the in-case-of-freak-out cable line. I tried to breathe deeply as tears of uncertainty rolled down my cheek.

After 30 minutes in the tube, I was wheeled out to wait for results. Fear wracked me; by now I was semi-certain I'd had a stroke. The doctor came in and without skipping a beat, she blurted out, "You have multiple sclerosis."

What? I was sure I'd heard wrong. *I had a stroke.*

There was a river of words from the doctor about what they'd found on the MRI. A nurse handed Mark discharge papers and suggested I follow up with a neurologist. We left at 4 a.m. I was tired, drug-fogged, confused.

News slowly got out. Emails, texts, phone calls, and Facebook posts started flooding in with love, concern, well wishes. Every time I tried to read about multiple sclerosis I had to stop.

I wanted a conclusive diagnosis.

Monday morning at 9 a.m. was the neurology appointment. After a visit with the doctor, and a review of the MRI, it was conclusive. I had MS. Dr. Zirelli showed me the lesions on my brain. Spots of gray matter that looked like larvae. I disassociated from everything in the room. My body. The words. The space around me.

What if I end up in a wheel chair? Or blind? Or unable to speak, or walk? What if I turn into a vegetable?

These realities had never been remote possibilities for my life.

So far out of left field.

So surreal.

I can't attach my name, Janna, to having this disease. MS. This is an entire other identity. An identity of someone with a substantial disease.

Yep! Another midlife identity setback, a "D" no less…

I hadn't even gotten familiar with the new identity that was trying to form.

Anger kicked in. *No posters. No ribbons. No fundraisers, 5Ks, or walks. I don't want any of that. Fuck.*

This identity cloak was like looking into a closet and seeing an ugly jacket that doesn't belong to me and being told I have to wear it.

I don't want to wear it. I am not *a fucking poster child. This is* not *my new identity.*

* * * * *

One of the brightest Oscar 2019 stories was Selma Blair's appearance in a beautiful dress with a custom-designed cane, and her statement that life with multiple sclerosis goes on. After being diagnosed with MS a few days before the Academy Awards, I received that link of her red-carpet photo rocking the gorgeous dress from at least a dozen friends.

Whether you use the disease's initials, MS, or its full name, I never knew what the funny sounding illness was.

Before getting a full scope of my diagnosis, I imagined a lot of scary scenarios: wheel chairs, inability to talk, and a life of pain and suffering. I had a lot to learn. Here are eight random but important things I've discovered about MS.

1. I don't feel my body is betraying me. Rather, based on the complexity of this disease, I feel it has its own passport. It's off doing its own thing in Thailand while I decided to go to Finland. I am a foreigner in my own skin. My life is going on,

my thoughts are going on, and separately, my body has traveled to unknown parts for unknown reasons. I'm not angry at it. I can't hold resentment over fate or chemistry. That won't help.

2. The age at which one gets MS matters. The younger one is, the tougher it is. I am 51. I'm considered old for this diagnosis. For all the things age brings, a slowed immune system is one of them and in this case, that's a gift. My prognosis is brighter than if I were younger. MS affects 400,000 people in the U.S. between the ages of 20 and 50. Ten thousand new cases are diagnosed every year. MS is two to three times more common in women than men.

3. The severity of any case of MS depends on how many lesions are on the brain, and if they're also on the neck and spine. MS harms brain, optic, and spinal cord nerves. This causes the symptoms of compromised motor skills. *Sclerosis* means scarring and individuals with MS develop multiple areas of scar tissue in reaction to nerve damage. The average number of lesions at diagnosis is 20 to 30 but people can have more. I have 16. The ones I have are big, however. My very good news is that no lesions were found on my neck or spine.

4. Healthcare coverage matters. I live in Oregon, and luckily, a month before my diagnosis, because of hard financial times, I had to make a switch to the Oregon Health Plan, which provides care to Oregon residents regardless of ability to pay for health insurance. Unbelievably fortunate timing. Thank you to Oregon and to all the early healthcare insurance advocates and pioneers who had vision for the need and access to healthcare. This diagnosis would have financially ruined me. For decades.

5. The steroids used to combat flare-ups are a bitch. I had a six-day course of one-hour steroid infusions. Nobody told me how rough they would be. How taxing they would be on my psyche. How strange I would feel. Steroids are necessary during a flare-up or a relapse, in order to reduce inflammation around a spot of nerve damage. They help me recover and abate the associated symptoms after a relapse. An exacerbation of MS can be mild or severe and cause new symptoms or make old symptoms worse. No two relapses are alike and symptoms vary person to person. Sometimes inflammation in the central nervous system affects speech, balance, or vision. Most people, including me, feel incredibly fatigued for days or even weeks afterward.

6. Treatment for MS has come a long way in the past 20 years—it's more effective and promising. Although nothing cures MS, there are more options than ever to halt and put the disease into remission.

7. I'll eventually have to change my diet. Dr. Terry Wahls, MS patient and advocate, has done Ted talks about how changing her diet saved her life. For now, I've started with a couple of important steps—taking vitamin B-12 and vitamin D, and getting a healthy dose of greens through juicing every day. Eventually, I'll have to follow a more paleo-style diet, which is anti-inflammatory. That will mean eating more greens and cutting out sugar, gluten, and dairy.

8. People are truly kind. There's a side of human nature that I never would have seen without this diagnosis. The phone calls, texts, and emails have been overwhelmingly heartfelt, uplifting, and extremely supportive. I was blown away by how generous people were. I definitely received a beautiful glimpse into the

compassion of the human heart during someone else's crisis. To know this generosity has been a gift.

Although I feel a kinship with Selma Blair because we're strangers united by a shared world, I'm that sad she or anyone has to ride this crazy MS train. I'm sad for me, too.

After intensive steroid treatments, way too many tears, and a chance for the shock dust to settle, here's the outlook: I have non-progressive, relapsing multiple sclerosis. My symptoms have been tingling hands and arms, cloudy vision, exhaustion, and a steady ringing in my ears. My prognosis is good. I had my first eight-hour infusion treatment. The drug is called Rituximab (which is sometimes used for certain cancers. It's been shown to be very effective in stopping MS progression and initiating remission.) I'll have infusions every six months for a few years, then once a year for a few years. Total treatment is nine years. I'll be (gasp!) 60 at the time of the last infusion.

Overall, I feel okay, and I'm slowly improving. Some days are better than others and I meander between physical, emotional, and mental impacts. I have no idea where this road will lead, but I'm optimistic. I'm aware that this medical crisis could be worse. I also want to reiterate in case it wasn't clear, by this point, Mark and I were on a promising healing path. And thank goodness. He was amazing, supportive and truly made me feel as if whatever was ahead wouldn't have to be faced alone. I remain grateful he hung in there with me.

As for my identity search and my notion of Self in midlife, the diagnosis not only radically shifted a presumed tidy ending of this book, it jettisoned me into an entirely new identity conundrum. I never saw myself as having a disease, let alone MS. But for some reason, I'm distanced from owning the label. Maybe that's a good thing. Thank goodness

I have health care. Thank goodness I have love. Thank goodness I have the luxury of hope.

And as the past few years have revealed, this is yet another mile marker spotlighting humble discovery along a continual pattern of Flight. Ha ha, the punchline's on Me—turns out there is no all-encompassing, grand-finale landing, as I'd idealized.

There are no predictable, or perfect, or tidy takeaways just waiting to soar off into a falsely contrived Hollywood sunset. This is it ...

as we are,

as it is,

for all we've got.

Can a tangled life fulfill enough?

It is assuring that there is some brighter, wiser light to help glide beyond midlife darkness. It allows the Flight to feel a little more free—and a little more like *Me*.

Acknowledgments

Here's where I get to feign I'm a surprised actress who's just won the Oscar. I'd like to thank…

First, Mark, my husband. This was a selfish endeavor and one I needed to see through. There were many personal aspects about my life and experience that brought Mark along as innocent bystander—yet, he allowed the entirety of the process, even at his own expense. There are no words to express the deeply held gratitude for his ongoing understanding and acceptance of Me, just as I am, always. Thank you for this, and for everything you are in my life. I learned the major life lesson about truest love, one without conditions, from you.

Thank you to my children for creating the meaning of life, and creating Me. I'm sorry I didn't always get it right, do it right, say it right, or show it right. I love you both so much. I hope these words can someday shed light on the flawed yet heart-centric humanness and complicated connection to motherhood. You are both gifted souls. My eternal love…

Thank you to my friends who showed up for happy hours, tears, phone calls, and french fries (Delila, Becki, Roxanne, Jana, Dawn, Julie, Audrey, Stephanie, L.E., Tascha, Tom, Vonie, Brenda, Holly, Mark R., Marty, Naomi, and Thomas).

Thank you to Hope Edelman, for helping me turn a writing corner,

Raphael, for your wisdom, heart and support,

Julie, for the encouragement and better words,

John, for being a constant touchstone,

Hafez, for your continued protection,

Santa Fe, for the sacred stillness,

my brother, who's there when needed,

my mom, whose kindness knows no limits,

my father, who was one-of-a-kind,

My grandma and grandpa, whose love is always with me.

And in no particular order, these influences and comforts that helped guide me in the darker days: hummingbirds, Bernie Taupin's beautiful masterpiece lyrics (to Elton John's music), my cats—Leo and Luna, beautiful sunsets, exceptional tequila, taking photos of pretty details, encouraging teachers including Jay Ponteri and Brandon Shimoda, the Multiple Sclerosis Society and their dedication to education, research and support, every individual who's supported and encouraged the writing of this book, and all the brave lost and lonely midlife souls out there trying to fly their way back. I love you.